Iris Kürschner

Vanoise

Albertville – Trois Vallées – Val d'Isère – Maurienne

Translated by Gill Round

52 selected day walks
in the Tarentaise, the Maurienne and the Vanoise National Park

With 97 colour photos,
52 small walking maps to a scale of 1:50,000 / 1:75,000 / 1:100,000
and an overview map to a scale of 1:550,000

ROTHER · MUNICH

Front cover:
Lac de la Croix high above the Col du Glandon.

Photo opposite the title page (page 2):
on the way to Basse de Gerbier at the foot of the Aiguilles d'Arves.

All photos by Iris Kürschner.

Cartography:
walking maps to a scale of 1:50,000 / 1:75,000 / 1:100,000
Kartografie Christian Rolle, Holzkirchen
Overview maps to a scale of 1:550,000 and 1:1.600,000
© Freytag & Berndt, Vienna

Translation:
Gill Round

The description of all the walks given in this guide are made according to the best knowledge of the author. The use of this guide is at one's own risk. As far as is legally permitted, no responsibility will be accepted for possible accidents, damage or injury of any kind.

1st edition 2005
© Bergverlag Rother GmbH, Munich

ISBN 3-7633-4829-8

Distributed in Great Britain by Cordee, 3a De Montfort Street, Leicester
Great Britain LE1 7HD, www.cordee.co.uk

ROTHER WALKING GUIDES

Algarve · Andalusia South · Azores · Bernese Oberland East · Corsica · Costa Brava · Costa Daurada · Côte d'Azur · Crete East · Crete West · Cyprus · Gomera · Gran Canaria · Iceland · La Palma · Madeira · Mallorca · Mont Blanc · Norway South · Provence · Pyrenees 1, 2, 3 · Sardinia · Sicily · High Tatra · Tenerife · Tuscany North · Valais East · Valais West · Vanoise · Via ferrata Dolomites · Via ferrata Switzerland · Zugspitze

Dear mountain lovers! We would be happy to hear your opinion and suggestions for amendment to this Rother walking guide.

BERGVERLAG ROTHER · Munich
D-85521 Ottobrunn · Haidgraben 3 · Tel. (089) 608669-0, Fax -69
Internet www.rother.de · E-mail bergverlag@rother.de

Foreword

Admittedly the Vanoise massif is not very well known outside of France, although names like Les Trois Vallées, Les Arcs and Val d'Isère will mean something to winter sports enthusiasts. But where are these places exactly? Tarentaise, Maurienne? Are they kinds of cheese? And yet a lot of people know the region from at least travelling along the famous Grande Route des Alpes as it winds its way across the highest passes of the French Alps from Geneva to Nice. At car parks, passes and selected viewing points I have met Austrians, Germans and Swiss who knew little more than that they were in the French Alps and were enthralled with the grandeur of the mountains, but didn't really have the confidence to venture out into the landscape. That's all going to change now with the aid of this hiking guide.

The 'Parc National de la Vanoise', the first national park in France, was originally established because of the rapid decline in ibex and chamois and today contains a large number of animals. Previously there were only 40 ibex scrambling across the high mountains, but today there are more than 1500. And 4700 chamoix also like to display their climbing skills. With such an abundance of animals it is worth taking a pair of binoculars with you, since it's not a rare occurrence to also come across black grouse and eagles. The unusually tame marmots who often construct their holes directly under the path, are creatures that can entertain the whole family. The geological diversity of the park is also fascinating and you will be amazed at the luxuriant plant life and countless crystal clear mountain lakes inviting you to take an invigorating swim.

The national park has some delightful mountain roads with wonderful views awaiting you at every bend – mountain glaciers, idyllic high valleys, gushing streams flowing down over colourful stones. It makes you long to go hiking right in the heart of the Vanoise mountains, for you can only discover these mountains on foot, and the possibilities for hiking are endless. There are altogether 500 waymarked hiking paths and 66 places of accommodation at your disposal for over 100 summits above the 3000m mark. Many of them are relatively easy to access for fit hikers which makes for a good choice of pleasurable summit ascents. However, this walking guide does not confine itself to walks in the national park. The delightful border regions are rarely frequented by the majority of hikers and many charming and more isolated routes are to be discovered there. Together with numerous moderately difficult panoramic and lake walks, there are also some easy walks and a few very challenging high mountain trails included to cater for a variety of walking preferences and degrees of fitness.

Spring 2005   Iris Kürschner

Contents

Foreword 5
Tourist tips 8
   Information 10
Hiking in the Vanoise 20
Contextualising map 26

Albertville
1. La Roche Pourrie, 2037m 28
2. Le Grand Arc, 2484m 30
3. Les Lacs de la Tempête, 2131m 32
4. Pierra Menta – Refuge de Presset, 2514m 34
5. Le Grand Plan, 2127m 38

Les Trois Vallées
6. Crève-Tête, 2341m 40
7. Grand Perron des Encombres, 2825m 42
8. Col de la Vallée Etroite, 2732m 44
9. Refuge du Saut – Lac du Mont Coua, 2672m ... 46
10. Lacs Merlet, 2449m 48
11. Petit Mont Blanc, 2677m 50
12. Crête du Mont Charvet – Col de la Grande Pierre, 2403m 52
13. Les Cirques de Pralognan 54
14. Refuge de Péclet Polset, 2459m – Lac Blanc, 2429m 58
15. Tour de l'Aiguille des Aimes 62
16. Pointe de la Vélière, 2467m 66
17. Mont Jovet, 2558m 68

Haute-Tarentaise
18. Porte de Rosuel – Lac de la Plagne, 2145m ... 70
19. Lancebranlette, 2936m 74
20. Lac du Retour, 2397m 76
21. Tour du Montséti 78
22. Col du Lac Noir, 2869m – Col du Rocher Blanc, 2833m 80
23. Glacier de la Savinaz, 2300m 82
24. Lac de la Sassière, 2460m 84
25. Col de la Rocheure, 2911m 86
26. Col de la Galise, 2987m 88

Haute-Maurienne
- 27 Refuge du Carro, 2759m ... 90
- 28 Cirque des Evettes, 2591m ... 92
- 29 Refuge d'Avérole, 2229m ... 94
- 30 Rochemelon, 3538m ... 96
- 31 Pierre aux Pieds, 2750m ... 100
- 32 Pointe de Lanserlia, 2909m ... 102
- 33 Plan du Lac – Sentier Balcon de l'Arpont ... 104
- 34 Le Sentier des Bâtisseurs ... 108
- 35 Via ferrata du Diable ... 110
- 36 La Turra – Trou de la Lune, 2650m ... 112
- 37 Pointe de l'Observatoire, 3015m ... 114
- 38 Le Rateau d'Aussois, 3131m ... 118

Maurienne
- 39 Signal du Petit Mont Cenis, 3162m ... 120
- 40 Lac de Savine, 2447m – Lacs Giaset, 2664m ... 122
- 41 Vallon d'Ambin – Pas de la Coche, 2968m ... 124
- 42 Mont Thabor, 3178m ... 128
- 43 Tour de la Fourche ... 132
- 44 Col des Aiguilles d'Arves, 3163m ... 134
- 45 Basse du Gerbier, 2578m ... 136
- 46 Cime de la Valette, 2858m ... 138
- 47 Glacier de St-Sorlin, 2715m ... 142
- 48 Lac de la Croix, 2415m – Col du Sambuis, 2528m ... 146
- 49 Mont Rond d'en bas, 1522m ... 148
- 50 Pic de Fremezan, 2261m ... 150
- 51 Grand Coin, 2730m ... 152
- 52 Rocher de Sarvatan, 2510m ... 154

Index ... 156
Glossary for mountain walkers ... 159

Tourist tips

Use of the guide
The description of the each walk is preceded by a fact-file section containing the most important information. A description of the route follows an introductory characterization of the walk. Particularly where there are clear paths with appropriate waymarkings, the description is kept as concise as possible and to the point. The small colour walking map contains the line of the route. In the index at the back can be found all the destinations, towns and villages, starting points and bases that are mentioned. The location of all the walks is marked on an overview map.

Due to an inadequate network of public transport, care has been taken to establish circular walks with an identical starting and finishing point. There are also suggestions for linking some of the them to form multi-day walks.

Grades
Most of the walks described in this book go along well marked paths, but sure-footedness and a level of fitness are often required because of the rugged terrain. The majority go across terrain where there are signposts as well as paint waymarkers. Only the national park confines itself, except for the white-red-white GR (Grande Randonnée/long distance paths), to well placed directional signs.

Your attention is drawn to special technical demands which are called for in certain individual walks, for example, on glacier crossings, sections of rock climbing, difficult parts of the path etc. To help you assess the grade of each walk at a glance the route numbers are marked in three different colours:

BLUE
Easy walks on well-marked, mostly broad hiking paths which, for the most part, are only moderately steep and hardly exposed at all. They do not require any mountain walking experience. These routes are also relatively danger-free in bad weather.

RED
Walks for more advanced walkers which require a certain amount of sure-footedness, a lack of vertigo and a certain level of fitness. Sturdy footwear is imperative. The paths are usually well marked, but at times narrow and exposed.

BLACK
Hiking paths and footpaths for seasoned mountain walkers who are sure-footed and very fit, have a head for heights and a good sense of direction. The routes are usually marked sufficiently well, but some sections could also be unmarked and without paths. They are often steep and exposed, and sometimes require the use of the hands (I, easy grade climbing).

Starting point (Walk 23) – the 'picture book village' of La Gurraz in the Haute-Tarentaise.

Getting there
The fastest way by car is from Paris along the A8 in the direction of Dijon. South of Dijon turn off onto the A6 in the direction of Lyon and from there onto the A 43 towards Chambéry. At the motorway junction beyond Chambéry get into the correct lane in the direction of Albertville, the gateway to the Beaufortain and the Tarentaise, or onto the A 43 into the Maurienne. This route is especially recommended for the fastest journey into the Maurienne.

If you have plenty of time, I recommend that you make the journey along the legendary Grande Route des Alpes from Geneva over the Col des Aravis (www.routedesgrandesalpes.com).

French motorways require you to pay a toll at each of the *péages*, prices varying depending on the length of each section of the road. You need a *vignette* on Swiss motorways which is obtainable at all border crossings, costs 40 Sfr. and is valid from 1.12. to 31.1. one year hence.

Travelling by public transport is complicated and requires several changes. Regular train and bus connections are only possible in the central valleys of the Tarentaise and the Maurienne. Bus services into the high and side valleys are rare and usually operate only during the short summer season in July and August.

Equipment
Sturdy walking boots with sticky soles and waterproof clothing. Sunglasses, sun cream and map. Food and drink, since there are few possibilities to stop and buy something to eat on the way. You should also take an emergency first-aid kit in the rucksack. Telescopic walking poles are helpful

INFORMATION

General

Maison de la France, 178 Piccadilly, W1J 9AL London, Royaume-Uni, ℂ 09068 24 41 23 (60 p/min. at all times), Fax 020 74 93 65 94, info.uk@franceguide.com, www.franceguide.com

Regional

Comité Régional du Tourisme Rhône-Alpes, 104, route de Paris, F-69260 Charbonnières-les-Bains, ℂ 04 72 59 21 59, Fax 04 72 59 21 60, rhonealpes.tourisme@wanadoo.fr, www.rhonealpes-tourisme.com

Agence Touristique Départementale de Savoie, 24, BD. de la Colonne, F-73025 Chambéry Cedex, ℂ 04 79 85 12 45, Fax 04 79 85 54 68, documentation@cdt-savoie.fr, www.savoie-tourisme.com

Parc National de la Vanoise, 135, rue du Docteur Julliand, F-73007 Chambéry, ℂ 4 79 62 30 54, www.vanoise.com

Haute Maurienne Informations, F-73480 Lanslebourg, ℂ 04 79 05 91 57, Fax 04 79 05 80 96, info@hautemaurienne.com, www. hautemaurienne.com

Offices du Tourisme in important places

F-73204 Albertville, Place de l'Europe, ℂ 04 79 32 04 22, Fax 04 79 32 87 09, tourisme@albertville.com, www.albertville.com

F-73500 Aussois, Maison d'Aussois, ℂ 04 79 20 30 80, Fax 04 79 20 40 23, info@aussois.com, www.aussois.com

F-73270 Beaufort, La Maison du Beaufortain, ℂ 04 79 38 37 57, Fax 04 79 38 31 56, E-Mail info@lebeaufortain.com, www.lebeaufortain.com

F-73480 Bessans, ℂ 04 79 05 96 52, info@bessans.com, www.bessans.com

F-73500 Bramans, ℂ 04 79 05 03 45, Fax 04 79 05 36 07, info@bramans-tourisme.com, www.bramans-tourisme.com

F-73480 Bonneval s/Arc, ℂ 04 79 05 95 95, Fax 04 79 05 86 87, info@bonneval-sur-arc.com, www.bonneval-sur-arc.com

F-73703 Bourg-Saint-Maurice, ℂ 04 79 07 04 92, www.bourgstmaurice.com

F-73260 Celliers, Syndicat d'Initiative, ℂ 04 79 24 36 34 or 04 79 24 05 05, Fax 04 79 24 38 48

F-73350 Champagny-en-Vanoise, ℂ 04 79 55 06 55, Fax 04 79 55 04 66, www.champagny.com

F-73122 Courchevel, ℂ 04 79 08 00 29, www.courchevel.com

F-73260 Grand Naves, Maison de la Montagne, ℂ 04 79 24 40 13, Fax 04 79 24 15 40

F-73480 Lanslebourg, Maison de Val Cenis ℂ 04 79 05 23 66

F-73480 Lanslevillard, Maison de Val Cenis, ℂ 04 79 05 99 10

F-73700 La Rosière-Montvalezan, ℂ 04 79 06 80 51, www.larosiere.net

F-73440 Les Menuires, ℂ 04 79 00 73 00, Fax 04 79 00 75 06, lesmenuires@lesmenuires.com, www.lesmenuires.com

F-73551 Méribel, ℂ 04 79 08 60 01, www.meribel.net

F-73500 Modane, ℂ 04 79 05 28 58, Fax 04 79 05 32 43

F-73600 Moûtiers, ℂ 04 79 24 04 23, www.ot-moutiers.com

F-73210 Peisey-Vallandry, ℂ 04 79 07 94 28, Fax 04 79 07 95 34, info@peisey-vallandry.com, www.peisey-vallandry.com

F-73710 Pralognan, ℂ 04 79 08 79 08, Fax 04 79 08 76 74, info@pralognan.com, www.pralognan.com

F-73130 Saint-Colomban-des-Villards, Maison du Tourisme de la Vallée des Villards, ✆ 04 79 56 24 53, Fax 04 79 59 14 38, villards@wanadoo.fr, www.saint-colomban.com

F-73640 Sainte-Foy-Tarentaise, ✆ 04 79 06 95 19, stefoy@wanadoo.fr

F-73530 Saint-Sorlin-d'Arves, ✆ 04 79 59 71 77, Fax 04 79 59 75 50, info@saintsorlindarves.com, www.saintsorlindarves.com

F-73130 St-Francois-Longchamp, ✆ 04 79 24 36 34, Fax 04 79 59 17 23, info@saintfrancoislongchamp.com, www.saintfrancoislongchamp.com

F-73440 St-Martin-de-Belleville, ✆ 04 79 00 20 00, Fax 04 79 08 91 71, stmartin@st-martin-belleville.com, www.st-martin-belleville.com

F-73500 Termignon, ✆ 04 79 20 51 67, Fax 04 79 20 51 82, info@termignon-la-vanoise.com, www.termignon-la-vanoise.com

F-73320 Tignes, ✆ 04 79 40 04 40, www.tignes.net

F-73155 Val d'Isère, ✆ 04 79 06 06 60, Fax 04 79 04 56, E-Mail info@valdisere.com, www.valdisere.com

F-73450 Valloire, ✆ 04 79 59 03 96, Fax 04 79 06 09 66, info@valloire.net, www.valloire.net

F-73260 Valmorel, ✆ 04 79 09 85 55, www.valmorel.com

**Up-to-date internet addresses can always be found on the website of Bergverlag Rother:
www.rother.de (WebLinks/GeoLinks).**

on steep ascents and descents. High alpine walks may require additional equipment and this is mentioned in the introductory information of the walk. It might also be useful to take along a small French dictionary if you don't speak the language.

Best season

Spring and autumn are the best time for stunning remote walks in the mountains. Despite the beautiful weather you will meet very few walkers as the French normally take their summer holidays from the middle of July to the middle of August. The drawback is that the tourist infrastructure outside of the short summer season runs at half mast, and in the major tourist centres, like Les Trois Vallée, even shuts down altogether. Nevertheless, most of the huts are staffed from the middle of June to the middle of September. Early in the year (June) you can expect to come across snowfields in the higher areas.

Literature/guides

- Walking in the Tarentaise and Beaufortain Alps, J.W.Akitt, Cicerone Press, 1995.
- Tour of the Vanoise, Kev Reynolds, Cicerone Press, 1996.
- Walking the French Alps: GR 5, Martin Collins, Cicerone Press, 2004.
- Vanoise Ski Touring, Paul Henderson, Cicerone Press, 2002.

In French:
- Topo Alpinisme Vanoise Haute-Maurienne, by Patrick Col,

The traditional costume dance in Bessans, the Haute-Maurienne, is pleasant to watch.

ISBN 2-9513938-1-4, extensive walking guide, every walk has a photo where the line of the route has been drawn in (also useful for non-French speakers), available from bookshops in the Haute-Maurienne and in the mountain guide office in Aussois.
- Vanoise, Massif et Parc national, Editions Didier Richard 2001, 94 walk descriptions without sketch maps.
- Circuits Pédestre Vanoise Haute-Tarentaise, guide franck 2002, by Marie-Geneviève Bourgeois, with removable route maps.
- Books in the series 'petites traces vertes', Editions Didier Richard, introduce 30 easy family walks. The following editions cover the region: Môutiers / Les Trois Vallées, Bourg-Saint-Maurice, Tignes / Val d'Isère, Val Vanoise, Maurienne.
- The national park offers special books and video cassettes: Oiseaux de Vanoise; Altitudes de Vanoise; Guide géologique du Parc national de la Vanoise, etc. The 40th birthday in 2003 was the reason for the special edition of a walking map 'La Carte' and a guide 'Le Guide' which also offers 40 walks together with some points of interest.

Protection of nature
It goes without saying that the Alps, the 'Playground of Europe', are put under an enormous strain and that every single 'mountain user' carries a joint responsibility – and, in particular, that everyone should take their rubbish away with them.

Special regulations are in force in the Vanoise National Park. Information boards at the park boundary explain the individual stipulations for protecting the park. Every man and woman is requested:
- to follow the hiking paths and not to take shortcuts
- not to pick flowers or fruit, or collect minerals
- to avoid disturbing the peace by making too much noise, shouting or playing music
- not to take dogs along (even if they are on a lead)
- to take all rubbish away
- not to camp (although basic tents are allowed near mountain huts under certain conditions and with a site payment in July and Aug.)
- not to light a fire
- to be aware that paragliding and mountain-biking are not allowed

Emergencies
Fire brigade, doctor and police work together in France. In the case of an emergency dial one of the following numbers: Pompiers ✆ 18; SAMU ✆ 15; Gendarmerie/Police ✆ 17. Mobile emergency number: ✆ 112.

Route finding
The directions 'left' and 'right' refer to the direction in which you are walking. On the other hand, any reference made to 'on the left/right hand bank', 'on the left/right hand side of the valley' always signifies 'in the direction of the water flow'.

Ibex are not unreasonably cautious.

Savoy specialities.

Specialities
Savoy is a paradise for lovers of cheese. A good selection of local cheeses is usually served after the main course, even in the huts. It's also a good idea to pack some cheese for the picnic – it tastes even better then – with a fresh *baguette* or some farmhouse bread, tomatoes, olives and, if it's not too heavy, perhaps a small bottle of wine.

The best cheeses made in Savoy are the creamy, piquant Reblochon, the hard cheese Beaufort, Serac, a strained white cheese and the mild Tomme de Savoie. 'Tomme' means nothing other than 'cheese' in Savoy. Cheese is also the basis of many local dishes. Fondue is popular as are various gratins, amongst them the world-famous Gratin dauphinois. But have you ever tasted Gratin savoyard, made with Tomme cheese? If this is all too much for you, simply order a snack, e.g. toast savoyard, crispy rye-bread with grated Reblochon and walnuts on top, or Tarte au Beaufort, a quiche that is served hot, filled with Beaufort and Crème fraîche. Tartiflette is one delicacy that surpasses all others. But you need a large appetite for this as a whole Reblochon cheese goes into the Tartiflette. The cheese is cut into thin slices and layered with potato, ham and spices, covered in crème fraîche and white wine, then lightly baked in a hot oven. Polenta is also served as the basis for various dishes or Crozet, noodles made with black flour. You should definitely leave room for dessert if there's bilberry tart, Tarte aux mures, or apple cake, Tarte aux pommes, on the menu.

Telephone
The dialing code to France is 0033; from France to England 0044. Mobile phones can be a problem as particularly deep valleys and gorges are bound to be black holes or provide only a weak signal.

Themed routes
A special feature around the Vanoise massif is the art historian treasures of numerous baroque churches and chapels which can be explored along the 'Chemins du baroque'. Information brochures about these can be obtained free from tourist offices.

Especially worth visiting amongst the churches in the Tarentaise are: the pilgrimage church of Notre-Dame-de-la-Vie at St-Martin-de-Belleville, Ancienne Basilique St-Martin in Aime, Notre-Dame-des-Vernettes at

One of the scenically most attractive sections of the Grande Route des Alpes is the narrow gorge of the Haute Tarentaise like here at Chervil.

Notre-Dame-de-la-Vie, St-Martin-de-Belleville.

Peisey-Nancroix and the Chapelle St-Grat-de-Vulmix at Bourg-St-Maurice; in the Maurienne: the Chapelle St-Antoine in Bessans, the Chapelle St-Sébastien in Lanslevillard, and the oldest church in Savoy, St-Pierre-d'Extravache in Val d'Ambin at Bramans.

There are also numerous forts to be found at the edge of the paths which are referred to as 'Pierres-fortes de Savoie' in the brochure of the same name.

Under the title of 'Route des Fromages' you will find an overview map that contains addresses and visiting times from cheese co-operatives.

Accommodation

- Auberge: reasonably priced inns with a typical regional menu, but not always with overnight accommodation.
- Chambres d'hôtes: a kind of bed & breakfast which is only to be found in this form in France. Most of them are idyllically located places of accommodation, often castles or pretty country houses. You can enjoy home cooking in the evening (the addition of table d'hôte symbolizes half board) in an informal atmosphere and you can practise your French a little and glean some local knowledge.
- Gîte d'Étape/Gîte de séjour: basic hiking accommodation, usually only with a bunkhouse, sometimes with rooms as well.
- Gîte rural: accommodation in country surroundings for families and self-catering (www.gites-de-france.fr).

■ Refuge: rustic mountain huts, usually only accessible on foot, often staffed by the French Alpine Club (CAF). The density of the huts in and around the Vanoise National Park is very good, mostly also the quality of the management (friendly atmosphere, often fresh food, local produce, mountain cheese etc.), if the hut is not already overcrowded. The huts are usually staffed from the middle of June to the middle of September, many also in the early part of the year for cross-country skiers. CAF places of accommodation have a winter room as well which is invariably open. Now and then you will also find huts for self-catering which are always open. The national park publishes the free magazine L'estive once a year which also contains, apart from up-to-date events, a handy list of huts with opening times and an overview map. You should phone ahead, in any case, to book in the high season of July and August.

■ Camping: campsites are to be found usually in the larger towns (www.camping-rhonealpes.de). Wild camping in the national park is strictly forbidden, but it's okay to do so outside its boundary and there are plenty of delightful spots.

Comprehensive brochures with addresses for all the individual types of accommodation are obtainable from the central tourist office of the Rhône-Alpes or Savoy.

Excursion organisers and clubs

An extensive tour program is usually offered by the local mountain guide offices, www.guides-savoie.com.

Refuge du Plan du Lac with Point de Lanserlia.

French hiking and mountaineering associations:
Fédération francaise de randonnée pédestre (FFRP), 64, rue de Gergovie, F-75014 Paris, ✆ 01 45 45 31 02, Fax 01 43 95 68 07.
Fédération Nationale des Clubs Alpins Francais (CAF), 24, avenue Laumière, F-75019 Paris, ✆ 01 53 72 87 00, www.clubalpin.com.

Buying food and petrol

On the whole, it is advisable to pack something to eat in your rucksack when out walking in the mountains. Something unexpected can always happen in the mountains, whether you have to shelter for a long time because of a thunderstorm or the route turns out to take longer than planned for various other reasons.

The huts in the hiking area are almost always several hours walking distance away from each other. Roadhouses are not usually available in between, but wonderful spots to stop for a bite to eat in the open air where everything tastes so much better, are in plentiful supply. Shopping in July and August is never a problem. There are small supermarkets and bakeries in every mountain village. These are, however, almost always closed outside the short high season and it is not unknown to have to walk miles out of your way to larger settlements. In the central valley of the Tarentaise and the Maurienne a supply of provisions is guaranteed all year round. So it is advisable, in the period between May and the middle of July, September and October, to do your food shopping before carrying on into the side valleys. Large supermarkets are often open during midday and on Sunday mornings and there's usually a petrol station close by. It makes sense to fill up with petrol if you get the chance (it will not be cheaper anywhere else) as petrol stations are relatively rare in the high valleys.

Walking maps

In France the best hiking maps are the blue IGN maps to a scale of 1:25,000 (called TOP 25). The official hiking paths and tourist sights are marked in red. However, not all the existing paths are included. This is where the IGN maps Alpes sans Frontières (sheets 12 to 15) have proved to be better, but they only cover the border area unfortunately. The maps are available locally in Maisons de la Presse, tobacco shops, bookshops, and often in tourist offices and bars as well.

Long distance paths

Two of the white-red-white marked long distance paths, so-called Grandes Randonnées (GR for short) run through the hiking area described in this book: the GR 5 (Amsterdam – Nice) and the GR 55 as an intersecting connection. If you put these together, you have two fabulous circular walks: Le Tour des Glaciers de la Vanoise, an absolute classic, which goes round the extensive glacial plateau in the heart of the Vanoise massif in seven stages;

Camping on the Col de la Croix de Fer with a view into the Arvan valley.

Le Tour de Méan Martin et du Grand Roc Noir, a four day walk through the eastern adjoining part of the national park. Folded sheets with a short description of each stage are free from information offices in the national park and also from local tourist offices. The topo guide to La Vanoise (Réf. 530) is very useful, published by the Fédération Francaise de la Randonnée Pédestre, with detailed descriptions, times and sections of maps, available from bookshops.

Weather
You can usually find the weather forecast (metéo) for the next few days on display in the tourist offices. General weather conditions in the Savoy can be obtained if you telephone ⓒ 08 92 68 02 73, mountain weather ⓒ 08 92 68 04 04, on the Internet www.meteo.fr.

Hiking in the Vanoise

The region covered in this guide
In actual fact it's quite easy to find the hiking area described in this book amongst the confusion of the French mountain ranges on the map as the area, enclosed by the Val d'Isère and Val d'Arc, has the unmistakable shape of a chicken and immediately catches your eye. It lies in the southernmost corner of the department of Savoie which belongs to France's largest region of Rhône-Alpes and shares a border with Italy in the southeast. The Vanoise National Park lies at the rear end of the 'chicken', the famous Trois Vallées, the largest skiing area in France, in the stomach of the 'chicken', the mountain range of Lauzière west of the Col de la Madeleine runs through the neck and on the cranium is Albertville, the former Olympic village. Not only the inside of the 'chicken' has interesting mountain walks, there's also a fascinating mountain scenery lying hidden around the edge, at times even more dramatic and remote. The 'chicken' and border areas share between them the Tarentaise, as the Val d'Isère is called, in the north, and the Maurienne, the Val d'Arc, in the south. Beak and head are bordered in the northwest by the Combe de Savoie.

Tarentaise
The upper course of the Isère with its side valleys is referred to as the Tarentaise. Savoy's second largest valley, for centuries an important traffic axis over the Col du Petit St-Bernard to Italy, is divided into three sections. The elongated gorge between Albertville and Moûtiers belongs to the Basse-Tarentaise. Between Moûtiers and Bourg-St-Maurice the valley widens out to the Moyenne-Tarentaise, then narrows again into a gorge, runs up Val d'Isère to the Col de l'Iseran and belongs to the Haute-Tarentaise. The Basse and Moyenne-Tarentaise are bordered in the north by the central ridge of Beaufortain. Deep valleys cut into the Vanoise massif to the south.

Moûtiers is the starting point for the well-known Trois Vallées, so called for marketing purposes since the skiing areas of Vallée de Belleville, Vallée d'Allues and Vallée de St-Bon are connected to one another and form the largest skiing area with a total of 400km^2. The resorts like Les Ménuires, Val Thorens, Méribel and Courchevel were created in the 30s and fortunately, no more development is allowed today. In the summer they become real ghost towns and seem out of place in relation to the spectacular mountain scenery roundabout. There is modest tourism from the middle of July to the middle of August. On the other hand, this is what makes the region more attractive as a remote hiking area, because once you have turned the right corner (and the Walks in this book tell you which is the right one), all the negative signs of winter tourism have disappeared.

The Moyenne-Tarentaise is characterized particularly by broad areas of forest and meadows in between tranquil villages. Tarentaise cattle are much prized here and are best suited to life in the mountains and provide spots of colour to the green pastures with their red coats. They are famous for their excellent milk from which the strong Beaufort cheese is produced, the king amongst the natural milk cheeses, which you should make a point of buying for your picnic from one of the cheese co-operatives or the supermarket. Bourg-St-Maurice is the intersection of three important alpine valleys with passes into Beaufortain, Italy and the Maurienne. You will not

You can recognize Beaufort cheese from its concave roundness.

get a more lively experience of the traditional costume of the region than at the Fête des Edelweiss which takes place every year in July when groups in traditional costume gather together from the Tarentaise and the neighbouring Aosta valley. The Frontière, the pretty yellow and black headdress of the Tarentaise women, is striking and has become the symbol for the whole of Savoy. After Bourg-St-Maurice the course of the Isère veers off to the south into the Haute-Tarentaise. This breathtaking section with ancient hamlets in the midst of verdent green and steep rock faces with cascading waterfalls is a section of the famous high trail of La Grande Route des Alpes, used chiefly by the majority of tourists as such. Some unbelievably beautiful walks can be found hidden at the higher levels. Then from the large reservoir at Tignes onwards, the Lac du Chevril, the natural landscape is behind you, at least along the side of the road. The huge ski area of Val d'Isère opens up after the Daille narrowing. But even here, with the right tips, there are some fabulous natural idylls to be discovered. Tourist products then come into their own and the walker can buy supplies, for there are hardly any supermarkets and bakeries between Bourg-St-Maurice and Val d'Isère. The road climbs round many long bends through barren mountainous country onto the Col de l'Iseran, with 2764 metres, one of the highest alpine passes and the border with Maurienne.

Maurienne

Val d'Arc, with 180km, the longest alpine valley in the Savoy, is referred to as the Maurienne. It runs from the Combe de Savoie in a wide loop from the west to the east, encompasses the southern part of the Vanoise massif and ends at the southern gateway of the Col de l'Iseran where its sources emerge in the Glacier des Sources de l'Arc. The lower part to St-Michel-de-Maurienne is marked by industrial complexes and workers' housing which stand in stark contrast to the fabulous mountain faces on the left and the right. At the same time one of the most important traffic axes runs through here to Italy. It ran previously over the Col du Mont-Cenis, but since 1980 the heavy traffic has fortunately disappeared, before Modane, through the Fréjus tunnel to the south. Another important transport link, but a rather more tourist form, is the Route du Galibier which connects the Maurienne with Briançonnais and is one of the most beautiful stages of the Grande Route des Alpes. The road from St-Jean-de-Maurienne winds its way up round innumerable bends to the Col du Télégraphe and runs through the scenically delightful valley of Valloirette. The tourist centre is Valloire and a good starting point for all kinds of walks. However, most visitors come in winter for the skiing and in summer it shuts down and becomes quiet and peaceful. The few hikers and mountaineers usually have only one aim – to get up close to the Aiguilles d'Arves whose three jagged pinnacles have become a symbol of the Maurienne. To the west another two still very unspoilt valleys cut into the mountains from the valley bottom of the Maurienne. The Arvan valley climbs to the foot of Grande Rousses and the Villards valley winds up below the north face of the Belledonne range of mountains. They are linked to one another over the Col du Glandon and the pass into Oisans. The so-called Haute-Maurienne begins after Modane, primeval and unspoilt compared to the lower Maurienne. There's modest tourism around La Norma, Aussois and Val Cenis, the skiing area of Lanslebourg and Lanslevillard. Majestic natural landscapes and small picturesque villages

Just before the Sources de l'Arc in the Haute-Maurienne.

retaining old customs make this a spectacular area.

Amongst the folk festivals of all kinds, the 'Fête de Dieu' is especially worth visiting in Aussois and takes place three times a year, twice at the end of June and on the 15. August as well. La Vierge Marie, the patron saint, is carried in a religious procession through the village accompanied by a troop of firework artists in Napoleonic costumes, folklore groups and women in traditional costumes. Bessans is

Marmot.

the centre of ancient folk art. The famous sacred figures were later replaced by the 'Diables de Bessans', grotesque demonic figures. One of the many legends tells how a local man once sold his soul to the devil who gave him 50 years of supernatural powers in return. When the pact came to the end the Bessan man travelled to Rome to ask the Pope for forgiveness. He was promised forgiveness if he went to three masses in three places a long way from each other. Thanks to the powers still being transmitted, he duped the devil, attended all three masses at the same time and so escaped hell. Woodcarvers of devils have a long tradition in Bessans. Georges Personnaz gladly opens up his studio in the Rue St-Esprit (side alley from the main square) and can tell you many legends about his little wooden devils. The last place in the Haute-Maurienne is Bonneval-sur-Arc, a real little picture-book village. The Italian province of Piemont borders directly onto the southern range of mountains.

The Vanoise National Park

The Vanoise National Park, founded in 1963, is the oldest national park in France. A cause for concern in the years beforehand was the rapid disappearance of alpine ibex and chamoix which were already being protected effectively in the neighbouring mountains of Gran Paradiso in Italy. Under pressure from organisations like the Club Alpin Francais, the Touring Club de France and hunting fraternity, the idea of establishing a national park became acceptable. Influential people also wanted the people in the border areas to be taken into consideration in order to preserve traditional village life. Eventually a two zone park was created. The tourist infrastructures are to be found in the large 1450km^2 border zone, the 'zone périphérique' – together with ancient mountain villages you will find the usual buildings associated with ski stations which are amongst the most important wintersport centres in France.

Sempervivum.

The actual area under protection, 'zone centrale', stretches just under 530km² across the whole of the Vanoise massif between Val d'Isère (Tarentaise) and Val d'Arc (Maurienne). It contains the largest mountain ranges of the region of which 107 peaks tower up over 3000m into the sky. The highest point is Grande Casse with 3855m in the heart of the massif. Other well-known peaks are Mont Pourri (3779m) and Sommet de Bellecôte (3416m) in the north, Grande Sassière (3747m) in the northeast, Grande Motte (3656m) in the centre, Pointe de la Sana (3456m) and Pointe de Méan Martin (3330m) in the east, Péclet-Polsetgroupe (3561m) and Dent Parrachée (3684m) in the south. Another 53km² of the region is covered by glaciers. Apart from mostly small glaciers, the ice mass is concentrated mainly on the huge Plateau of the Glaciers de la Vanoise between the Col de la Vanoise and the Col d'Aussois.

The geological diversity is enormous (limestone, gypsum, sand stone, quartz, slate, mica schist, gneiss), externally visible in the large variety of colours of the rock. From this structure has resulted a diverse flora as well. Amongst over a thousand different species of plants there are also Mediterranean species to be found, together with the common species. Here and there even some arctic-alpine relics have been able to survive from the ice age. Luxuriant carpets of gentian, edelweiss, anemones, alpine roses, mountain cowslips and saxifrage almost belong to the everyday picture in the warm summer months. Countless orchids like early purple orchid and black vanilla orchid are especially beautiful during spring in the mountains. Other botanical gems are the different kinds of rock jasmine, aquilegia and sedge, cortusa, alpine forget-me-not (Eritrichium nanum), blue thistle and turk's cap lily. In the lower areas of vegetation you will find beautiful forests with spruce, pines, larch and stone pines, amongst them also rare downy oak.

Since the massif has been protected, the fauna has also recovered. The number of ibex has risen from only 40 to about 1500, today a third of the whole French population. The new generation of chamoix is also remarkable and has risen from 400 to about 4700 of these agile mountain acrobats. The park is especially famous for its numerous marmots as well which often lose all their shyness in the protected areas and even allow themselves to be fed at times. Just as easy to see are hares and various types of vole. It's more difficult to catch sight of foxes, badgers, martens, pine martens and stoats. There are also several types of bat, like the dwarf bat or the brown long-eared bat, which exist in the national park. In the bird world you will come across golden eagle, rock ptarmigan, grouse, rock partridge, eagle owl, owl, black woodpecker, three-toed woodpecker, rock blackbird, black flycatcher, wall creeper, crossbill, snow finch and of course the cheeky alpine chough. The lammergeyer has found a home here again after the reintroduction program in 1986. The many lakes and high moors are refuge for alpine newts, marsh toads and red frogs. Amongst the reptiles are to be found wood lizard, Smooth viper, Aesculapian viper and asp viper. The huge insect world is not covered scientifically at all in some parts. The apollo butterfly is an example of the 'Beaus'.

There are 66 places of accommodation at the hiker's disposal in the park. Five of them have been set up additionally as information centres and are called Portes du Parc (gates to the park). They are to be found at the edges of the protected zones and are easily accessible by road: Le Bois in the high valley of Champagny, Rosuel after Peisey-Nancroix, both reachable from the Tarentaise; L'Orgère via Villarodin-Bourget, the Fort Marie-Christine at Aussois and the Plan du Lac in the high vally of Termignon, are reachable from the Maurienne.

Since 1972, the national parks of Vanoise and Gran Paradiso have come together to set up a partnership programme across the border. With their total surface area of 125,000km^2, they form the largest protected area in Europa.

Ibex.

1 La Roche Pourrie, 2037m

High viewing point above Albertville

Col des Cyclotouristes – Blockhaus des Têtes – Roche Pourrie – Haut du Pré – Col des Cyclotouristes

View across Albertville.

Starting point: Col des Cyclotouristes, 1330m, 12km from Albertville. Approach along the D 105 via Conflans in the direction of Fort du Mont, then another 2km. Car park and picnic area with fresh water and info board.
Walking times: Col des Cyclotouristes – Blockhaus des Têtes 1 hr., Blockhaus des Têtes – Roche Pourrie 1 hr., Roche Pourrie – Haut du Pré 1¼ hrs., Haut du Pré – Blockhaus du Laitelet – Col des Cyclotouristes ¾ hr.; total time 4 hrs.
Height difference: 810m.

Grade: problem-free walk, steep ascent up the hillside for the most part through a shady wood.
Food: none.
Accommodation: Gîte de Molliessoulaz (with view of Mont Blanc), about 6km from the Col des Cyclotouristes in the direction of Queige, ✆ 04 79 38 02 58.
Alternative: there's also a direct start from the Gîte de Molliessoulaz along the yellow and red marked long distance path 'Tour du Beaufortain', 3½ hrs. up to the summit.
Map: IGN TOP 25, sheet 3432 ET Albertville.

La Roche Pourrie, the most western buttress of the Beaufortain main ridge, is a fantastic viewpoint. The view extends far across the deeply indented Val d'Isère to the peaks of Lauzière in the south, in the west the broad valley basin of Albertville with the Chartreuse and Bauges massifs, in the north the striking Aravis mountain chain with the pyramid-shaped Mont Charvin. Some interesting fortifications are to be found on the extensive hillside of the Forêt d'Albertville. The Fort du Mont, on a viewing point below the Col des Cyclotouristes, once controlled the strategically important Albertville where four valleys meet: the Tarentaise, the valley of Doron de Beaufort, the Arly valley and the Combe de Savoie. While troops and munitions were stationed in the fort, the Blockhaus des Têtes, a level higher and situated along the hiking trail, allowed an overview as an observation post across the high mountain ranges.

From the **Col des Cyclotouristes**, 1330m, go along the yellow marked forest path, taking shortcuts across the bends of a forest path, steeply uphill to the east to the **Blockhaus des Têtes**, 1650m. Together with the fort ruins you will find an idyllic picnic spot. Descend a short way to the forest road and info board. From there continue ascending directly through forest and across carpets of bilberry. A huge wooden figure, 'Le Géant du Petit Pré', is passed. The creatively chiseled giant is there to remind you about environmental protection – hikers should keep quiet as they walk across the mating ground of black grouse here. They are an endangered species. Soon the forest opens out. On the left below lies the broad meadows of the alpine meadow Haut du Pré. A path leads on the right of the wooded southwestern ridge towards Roche Pourrie, but then it ends on its southern face. It's better to go on the left around the start of the ridge and ascend on the northwest side along a clear path to the summit of **Roche Pourrie**, 2037m.

From the summit go eastwards along the ridge until the yellow and red marked hiking trail of the 'Tour du Beaufortain' comes across. Follow this path to the left down the slope as far as the clearing of Les Chappes, 1595m. Go left across open meadows to the **Haut du Pré** alpine hut, 1697m, then continue along the field path to the edge of the forest. Go right through the forest to another forest road, 1448m, which leads past the Blockhaus du Laitelet, 1361m, and back to the **Col des Cyclotouristes**.

29

2 Le Grand Arc, 2484m

One of the best panoramic views which you have to work hard for

Le Champeney – Le Marret – Le Petit Arc – Le Grand Arc and back

Starting point: Le Champeney, 1140m, car park, mountain hut with fresh water, info board. Approach from Albertville along the D 925 to Ste-Hélène-sur-Isère (10km), then 6km to Bonvillard (D 69). After the church go left in the direction of La Léchère. After 1.5km go right and 4km through the wood to Le Champeney.
Walking times: Le Champeney – Le Marret 2½ hrs.; Le Marret – Le Petit Arc 1¼ hrs.; Le Petit Arc – Le Grand Arc 1 hr.; return 2¾ hrs.; total time 7½ hrs.
Height difference: 1350m.
Grade: sweat-inducing, steep ascent and descent, only for strong knees. There could still be some patches of old snow at the beginning of June.
Food: none.
Accommodation: the mountain huts of Le Champeney and Le Marret offer fairly neglected emergency accommodation; nearest accommodation: Hôtel le Sainte Hélène, Zone de Vernay, Ste-Hélène-sur-Isère, ✆ 04 79 38 43 72.
Alternative: the approach from Maurienne also has very beautiful views. Drive from Randens at the start of the Arc valley along the D 72 via Montsapey as far as the hamlet of Lieulever, 1250m. Ascent via the Col des Génisses, 1950m, and Lac Noir, 2014m, to the Petit and Grand Arc; descent via Char de la Turche, 2010m, and the Alpages du Chenalet, 1883m, back to the starting point; total time about 7 hrs. The strenuous ascents and descents demand a good degree of fitness and sure-footedness.
Map: IGN Top 25, sheet 3432 ET Albertville.

The massive mountain range which separates the Tarentaise from the Maurienne and the Combe de Savoie culminates in Grand Arc. The ascent from the Combe de Savoie through the extensive high forests is strenuous, but once at the top you are rewarded with idyllic high plateaus and a breathtaking panorama – from the Bauges massif in the west to the table mountains of Chartreuse, from the rugged serrations of the Belledonne mountain chain in the southwest to the glistening white peaks of the Grandes Rousses, the mountainous world of the Vanoise National Park beyond the Lauzière mountain chain in the east, then the icy peak of Mont Blanc, which attracts your attention in the north above the high ranges of Beaufortain. You are not alone amidst all this splendour – innumerable ibex also seem to be enjoying their surroundings.

At the **Le Champeney** info board, 1140m, go left up along the forest path. On the first right hand bend follow the unclear path straight ahead. Go steeply up the wooded hillside. Past a spring and crossing several forest paths you come to **Les Teppes**, 1610m. Go to the left around the clearing. At a fork (left goes to Les Michellettes) go right still quite steeply up to the turn-off for Lac de la Motte. To the left here and eastwards, cross a small high valley. Leave the small mountain hut, the **Chalet du Marret**, 1850m, on the left and continue across meadows, then through bushes of alpine rose steeply up beside the stream onto a small high plateau with several pools. Keeping right, climb up towards the ridge running down from the west. Follow the line of the ridge at first moderately ascending, then very steeply up across the western slope onto the pre-summit of **Le Petit Arc**, 2365m. Continue along the ridge to the summit cross of **Grand Arc**, 2484m. Return the same way.

View from Grand Arc of Mont Blanc.

3 Les Lacs de la Tempête, 2131m

A pass with a view of Mont Blanc and a high valley full of lakes

La Grande Maison – Col de la Louze – Les Lacs de la Tempête and back

Starting point: La Grande Maison, 1629m. Approach from Albertville or Moûtiers along the N 90, Sortie 37 (exit), then D 93 via Petit Coeur in the direction of Naves. On a sharp right hand bend with info board 'Alpages de Feissons', 1090m, turn left onto the forest road which bends round into the Vallée de la Grande Maison and after the Pont de la Fougère (5km) becomes a gravel track. A further 4km bumpy drive to the La Grande Maison car park with info board.
Walking times: La Grande Maison – Col de la Louze 1½ hrs., Col de la Louze – Les Lacs de la Tempête a good ¼ hr. to the first, another ½ hr. to the last lake; return 1½ hrs.; total time 3¾ hrs.
Height difference: 500m.

Grade: the strenuous ascents and descents on narrow paths demand a level of fitness and sure-footedness. You can expect to find patches of old snow at the beginning of June.
Alternatives: 1) Detour from La Grande Maison to the Lac du Plan du Jeu, situated on a high terrace to the northwest, 1¼ hrs. 2) If you do not want to entrust your car to the 4km long gravel track as far as La Grande Maison, park beyond the Pont de la Fougere which makes the walk 2 hrs. in total. Or start directly from Grand Naves: 3½ hrs. to La Grande Maison and 2½ hrs. back, making it 9½ hrs. in total.
Food: none
Map: IGN Top 25, sheet 3532 OT Massif du Beaufortain. Moûtiers. La Plagne.

Idyllic high terraces and secluded small valleys characterize the south side of the Beaufortain central ridge although this is not so evident on the drive through the lower Tarentaise since the dense covering of forest on the steep hillsides obstruct all views. Small quiet mountain roads climb up round numerous bends. A journey into the upper reaches of the valley is more than worthwhile. Pretty villages and picturesque hiking paths typify this forgotten corner of the world. The Col de la Louze is the name of the pass crossing between the Tarentaise and the Beaufortain and a section of the Tour du Beaufortain. The idyllic Lacs de la Tempête are espe-

Resting by the Lacs de la Têmpete.

cially popular at weekends. While most hikers approach from Lac de St-Guérin, the climb up from the Tarentaise is distinguished by its remoteness. On undulating meadows in between glistening lakes, burbling brooks and large boulders there are to be found marvellous picnic spots where children will find an exciting playground area.

From the car park at **La Grande Maison**, 1629m, follow the field path into the valley, over a stream (flowing in the spring) and go round a loop to the right to the alpine mountain hut of **La Carré**, 1710m. A marvellous view opens up here of the deeply indented valley. Continue further left northwards into the mountain cleft which leads up to the pass. Go along small tracks across the alpine meadows, then past some ruins, steeply up to the **Col de la Louze**, 2119m. There's a delightful view to the north of the Beaufortain with Lac de St-Guerin. The brilliant white massif of Mont Blanc towers up behind that. The yellow and red marked path to the left (west) continues below the southern precipices of Grand Mont across the boulder fields to the **Lacs de la Tempête**, 2131m. Return the same way.

4 Pierra Menta – Refuge de Presset, 2514m

Breathtaking ridge path for experienced walkers

Laval – Refuge de la Coire – Col du Coin – Roc de la Charbonnière – Pierra Menta – Refuge de Presset – Lac d'Amour – Refuge de la Coire – Laval

Starting and finishing point: Laval, 1650m; alpine settlement on the D 218, approach from the Tarentaise via Granier, 1240m. Also possible to continue along a gravel track to the Refuge de la Coire (the walk is then 2½ hrs. shorter).

Walking times: Laval – Refuge de la Coire 1½ hrs., Refuge de la Coire – Col du Coin 1½ hrs., Col du Coin – Roc de la Charbonnière 2 hrs., Roc de la Charbonnière – Pierra Menta 1 hr., Pierra Menta – Refuge de Presset ¾ hr., Refuge de Presset – Lac d'Amour 1½ hrs., Lac d'Amour – Refuge de la Coire 1½ hrs., Refuge de la Coire – Laval ¾ hr.; total time 10½ hrs.

Height difference: 1700m.

Grade: the ridge path Cormet d'Arêches – Col du Coin is not difficult, the continuation to Pierra Menta, however, is extremely exposed and only for surefooted mountain walkers with a head for heights. It is advisable to take crampons with you which can be used not only across snowfields, but also on precipitous grassy and gravel slopes. Only undertake in good weather conditions. If it's wet or there's too much snow, you are also ill-advised to undertake the walk. The ridge path from the Col du Coin is only marked with cairns.

Food and accommodation: Refuge de la Coire, ✆ 04 79 09 70 92 or 06 82 12 40 42; Refuge de Presset, ✆ 06 87 54 09 18; both staffed 15. June to 15. Sept.

Alternative: if you do not feel confident on the ridge section from the Col du Coin to Pierra Menta, it's advisable to take the shorter route over the Col du Coin with a detour to the idyllic Lac d'Amour, 6 hrs. in total.

Map: IGN Top 25, sheet 3532 OT, Massif du Beaufortain. Moûtiers. La Plagne.

Tip: trekking guide with more detailed route description: La Haute Route du Beaufortain by Jacques Maurin, obtainable from Maison du Beaufortain or local bookshops (unfortunately only in French).

The ridge path described here is only a short section of the Haute Route du Beaufortain which was opened in summer 2003 and runs spectacularly across the highest mountain ridges in 8 daily stages around the Beaufortain. The most spectacular section has been selected, full of bizarre rock towers and pillars, dramatic views into the far distance and down into the valleys. Because this small area contains such an extraordinary variety of rock , it is also a fascinating journey through geological history. The main attraction of the route is clearly Pierra Menta, a huge obelisk which proudly displays its magnificent form from every angle. Other gems are the turquoise Lac d'Amour, 'the lake of love', which lies embedded at the foot of Pierra Menta and the deep blue Lac de Presset in its dolomitic-type rock basin: an enchanting spot for those wishing to camp.

Lac d'Amour – idyllically located as it should be for a lake with this name.

Pierra Menta with the Refuge du Presset.

From the alpine mountain huts of **Laval**, 1650m, first follow the drivable track for a while until the hiking path turns off left before the bridge. Go up past the Chapelle St-Guérin to the **Refuge de la Coire**, 2059m. Then go a short way along the track to the **Cormet d'Arêches** pass, 2109m. A yellow waymarked hiking path with wonderful views now runs to the right up the ridge via **Croix du Berger** and **Mont Coin**, 2539m. Lac de St-Guérin lies at your feet embedded in the mountain chain of Beaufortain. On Mont Coin, Mont Blanc emerges into view. There's now a gentle descent onto the **Col du Coin**, 2398m. Continue following the ridge along obvious tracks to the east. After two conspicuous crags do not climb up onto the third one, go round it on the right instead and onto a col. Here you can either choose to go up the steep scree slope on the left or follow the path crossing a slope round to the right. Then ascend the grassy hillside before the steep gully up to the ridge. Continue along tracks across scree towards **Roc de la Charbonnière**, 2738m, then on the left of the northeastern ridge, at times along extremely exposed ledges, later on the right of the ridge, to the obelisk of **Pierra Menta**, 2714m. Go round this on the left across boulder fields and again onto the ridge with the many small rock pillars. On the other side descend steeply along some tracks and cross over to the yellow and red marked hiking path which leads to the **Refuge de Presset**, 2514m, which has been visible for quite a while. From the Refuge de Presset return the same way to the ridge at the foot of the northern face of Pierra Menta.

Go to the right on the other side round the large boulder field in a loop, then steeply across grassy slopes to **Lac d'Amour**, 2248m, lying in the west. Past its eastern shore ascend a small valley and make a long traverse over to the **Col du Coin**, 2398m. Descend northwestwards via the alpine mountain huts of Plan Brunet, 2205m, to the **Refuge de la Coire**, 2059m. Return along your ascent path to the car park at **Laval**.

5 Le Grand Plan, 2127m

Viewing point in the chamois reserve of Lauzière

Refuge le Logis des Fées – Lac de l'Arpettaz – Le Grand Plan – Lac du Branlay – Refuge le Logis des Fées

Starting point: Refuge le Logis des Fées, 1839m. Accessible along the 5km small mountain road 1km after Celliers on the northern road to the pass (D 94) to the Col de la Madeleine.

Walking times: Refuge le Logis des Fées – Lac de l'Arpettaz – Le Grand Plan 1 hr., Le Grand Plan – Lac du Branlay – Refuge le Logis des Fées 1 hr.; total time 2 hrs.

Height difference: 350m.

Grade: mountain walk suitable for families, with two short steep sections.

Food and accommodation: Refuge le Logis des Fées, staffed 15.6.–1.10., open all year round if you make a reservation, ✆ 06 82 17 06 34; Auberge du Glacier in Celliers-Dessus, ✆ 04 79 24 05 82; Hôtel du Grand Pic, in Celliers, ✆ 04 79 24 03 72.

Map: IGN Top 25, sheet 3433 ET, St-Jean-de-Maurienne. St-Francois-Longchamp. Valmorel.

On the way to Grand Plan you pass the pretty Lac de l'Arpettaz.

Starting point and accommodation with good views – the Refuge le Logis des Fées.

A really wonderful route goes across the Col de la Madeleine with pretty villages and a magnificent view of Mont Blanc. And when you have driven over the pass before, perhaps you have always thought of stopping here sometime to enjoy the fascinating terraced landscape on a leisurely walk below the Lauzière mountain chain. The Refuge le Logis des Fées provides you with accommodation with beautiful views, the nearby lakes invite you to take an invigorating swim and the high plateau of Grand Plan is simply enchanting with its open view of Mont Blanc, Vanoise, Meije and Lauzière. A large chamois reserve is situated just to the north as well (don't forget your binoculars).

From the **Refuge le Logis des Fées**, 1839m, continue along the roadway that is closed to private vehicles, which leads round wide bends to **Lac de l'Arpettaz**, 1961m, 1km away. Grand Pic de la Lauzière is reflected in the pretty little lake, while a view of Mont Blanc accompanies you in the north. From the lake climb the meadowed ridge westwards up to the left until you meet some obvious tracks. Zigzag steeply up southeastwards onto the dome of **Grand Plan**, 2127m.

Continue westwards across the undulating plateau of meadows with several pools into the valley basin with the **Lac du Branlay**, 2027m, visible from a distance. Follow the mountain path from the lake down the valley. The access to the **Refuge le Logis des Fées** is on the left just before the road.

6 Crève-Tête, 2341m

An easy ridge with great views

Refuge des Bachals – Refuge de Pierre Larron – Crève-Tête – Col du Gollet – Refuge des Bachals

Starting and finishing point: Refuge des Bachals, 1617m. Approach from the Morel valley, turn off from the D 95a at the hamlet of Le Pré to the left via La Charmette, later an unmade forest road.
Walking times: Refuge des Bachals – Refuge de Pierre Larron ½ hr., Refuge de Pierre Larron – Crève-Tête 2 hrs., Crève-Tête – Col du Gollet – Refuge des Bachals 1 hr.; total time 3½ hrs.
Height difference: 724m.
Grade: ideal family walk, with the only short tricky steep section on the descent from the Crève-Tête to the Col du Gollet.

Food: none.
Accommodation: hotels in the Morel valley. A overnight stay in one of the two self-catering huts Refuge de Pierre Larron and Refuge des Bachals is a rustic experience, always open, with stove and mattresses.
Alternative: approach also possible from the Belleville valley (access road via Fontaine-le-Puits): from the Col de la Coche via the Refuge Communal de Lachat. Another 1½ hrs.
Map: IGN Top 25, sheet 3433 ET, St-Jean-de-Maurienne. St-Francois-Longchamp. Valmorel.

A striking grassy ridge separates the valleys of Morel and Belleville. A ridge up to its highest point, the Crève-Tête, is easy to climb and with beautiful

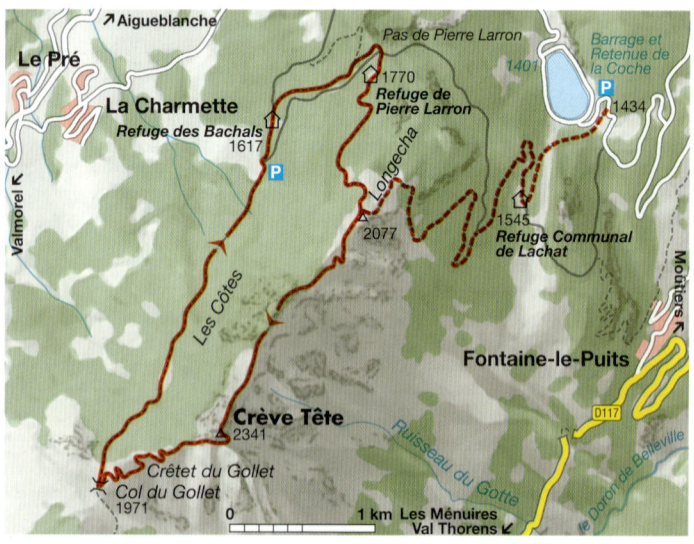

View of Cheval Noir from Crève-Tête.

views from the top. The Vallée du Morel lies in the west at your feet, with its last 'village', the resort of Valmorel. The granite peaks of the Lauzière mountain chain tower above and the Vallée des Belleville extends on the other side of the precipice. The glaciated peaks of the Vanoise massif line the horizon. From the **Refuge des Bachals**, 1617m, a path turns off from the drivable track to the east, crosses the roadway a bit higher up and later on reaches the clearing in the forest with the **Refuge de Pierre Larron**, 1775m. Go up the field path there on the left. Then go right onto the path that leads up a steep incline at first through forest, eventually across open terrain onto the start of the ridge. **Longecha**, 2077m, the area of meadows ribbed with rock, already offers the first impressive views especially into the deeply indented Val d'Isère in the east. There's another short steep incline until the line of the ridge is finally reached. Follow this to the summit cross of **Crève-Tête**, 2341m.

From the summit cross go a few metres down the eastern side, then round a wide bend to the west around the rise of the summit and along a tricky zig-zag path across the southern side which shows signs of a landslide. Go along below the descending grassy ridge onto the **Col du Gollet**, 1971m. Cross over to the right a long way through bushes and back to the **Refuge des Bachals**.

7 Grand Perron des Encombres, 2825m

A historic crossing over a pass and a peak full of ibex

Les Frachettes – Planlebon – Caseblanche – Refuge de Gittamelon – Petit Col des Encombres – Grand Perron des Encombres – Refuge de Gittamelon – Les Priots – Les Frachettes

Starting point: Les Frachettes, 1445m, in the Vallée des Encombres, 2km from Châtelard and 4km from St-Martin-de-Belleville (bus service to Moûtiers/station). Car park on the right below the road.

Walking times: Les Frachettes – Planlebon – Refuge de Gittamelon 1½ hrs., Refuge de Gittamelon – Caseblanche 1 hr., Caseblanche – Petit Col des Encombres 1 hr., Petit Col des Encombres – Grand Perron des Encombres 1½ hrs., return 4 hrs.; total time 9 hrs.

Height difference: about 1550m.

Grade: not a difficult mountain walk, but one which demands a level of fitness and in the summit area, you need to be very surefooted, a tricky passage just before the summit is made safe with a cable.

Food and accommodation: Refuge de Gittamelon, staffed July/Aug., ✆ 04 79 08 91 46.

Map: IGN Top 25, sheet 3433 ET, St-Jean-de-Maurienne. St-Francois-Longchamp. Valmorel.

Tips: in order to shorten this walk you can drive directly to Gittamelon (4km) or even to Caseblanche (8km) (bumpy gravel track!). The Circuit de Planlebon is also a worthwhile walk in itself: 3 hrs.

The pilgrimage church of Notre-Dame-de-la-Vie at St-Martin-de-Belleville. Restaurant Le Montagnard in St-Martin-de-Belleville, a former stable which has been renovated in a rustic style with specialities of the region, e.g. paillasse (a special kind of rösti).

If you look at leaflets about the Vanoise you will always come across a photo where herds of ibex are sunning themselves on the summit of Grand Perron des Encombres. This picture is incredibly motivating and makes you want to stand on the summit yourself. But be careful – if you do not reach the top by midday, you might be looking in vain for these proud animals since, by then, the herd has usually moved somewhere into the cool shade. The ascent starts eventfully through a dramatic gorge along the Circuit de Planlebon, then runs fairly persistently into the head of the valley where you have to put up with the crackling of electric power lines here and there. The landscape gets more exciting again of nature from the Petit Col des Encombres onwards.

From the car park of **Les Frachettes**, 1445m, cross the sloping meadow to the southwest and steeply descend through the forest down to the Encombres mountain stream which crashes through a deep crevice at the bridge. A zigzag path on the other side takes you to the old chapel of

Planlebon. Go left along a meadow path up the valley by the stream. After crossing three side streams change over onto the other side of the valley and ascend up to the refuge of Gittamelon, 1674m. Go along the road to the right as far as the bridge of **Caseblanche**, 1859m. Carry straight on before the bridge. The broad path at first runs through the valley bottom of the Ruisseau de Maubec, leaving the alpine mountain huts on the right, then onto the broad mountain ridge from where you can look down across the whole valley. Go along the ridge to the south onto the **Petit Col des Encombres**, 2329m. From the col go to the right onto the southeastern slope of Grand Perron des Encombres. Go left round a conspicuously jutting rock. At its southern foot you come to a board giving information about the animal species. Continue to the west towards the ridge between Petit Perron and Grand Perron. Go right for a short way along the ridge, then steeply across the loose gravel of the southeastern hillside, at the last moment secured with a cable, onto the summit of **Grand Perron des Encombres**, 2825m, with an orientation board. Go back the same way to just before **Gittamelon**, 1674m, where your previous ascent path branches off left. Then continue straight ahead following the yellow marked Circuit de Planlebon to Gittamelon. This path turns off left from the road just after the village and leads via the hamlet of **Les Priots**, 1596m, back to the starting point.

8 Col de la Vallée Etroite, 2732m

Idyllic lakes in the middle of a major skiing area

Les Bruyères – Lac de Lou – Lacs de Pierre Blanche – Col de la Vallée Étroite – Les Bruyères

Starting and finishing point: Les Bruyères, 1758m, old hamlet below Les Menuires on the road to Val Thorens.

Lac de Lou.

Walking times: Les Bruyères – Lac de Lou 1 hr., Lac de Lou – Lacs de Pierre Blanche 1½ hrs., Lacs de Pierre Blanche – Col de la Vallée Etroite 1½ hrs., return 2½ hrs.; total time 6½ hrs.
Height difference: 1000m.
Grade: some steep ascents.
Food: Restaurant Les Sonnailles in Les Bruyères; Buvette Refuge du Lac de Lou; Chalet d'alpage La Chasse, ✆ 06 09 45 28 35, where you can watch them doing the milking and making cheese and give a helping hand.
Accommodation: Refuge du Lac de Lou, July/Aug. and booking by telephone, ✆ 06 12 20 61 44.
Alternative: the Lac de Lou in itself is a marvellous and very popular day out for the family. With the return via La Chasse, it makes a nice circular walk (2¼ hrs. in total).
Maps: IGN Top 25, sheet 3433 ET St-Jean-de-Maurienne and sheet 3534 OT Les Trois Vallées. Modane; Carte des Sentiers Vallée des Belleville, 1: 33,333, with numbered walking list, obtainable from tourist offices.

What a contrast! The old hamlet of Les Bruyères with its weathered stone walls, and above it the resort of Les Menuires, as if taken from George Orwell's vision of the future. The bell tower sticks out – a symbol of this modern ski station. The bells sound every hour on the dot even if there's no one around to hear them. The town is fairly dead outside the winter season and the hotel towers only come alive with a few tourists in July and August. Families like to come here. Many of the walking paths are easy and well signposted. The goats gambol around the rustic alpine huts of La Chasse and you can learn how to milk them and take part in making cheese.

Lac de Lou is a particular gem, only one hour's walk away and completely out of sight of the extremes of civilization. Wild streams rush down the mountain slopes, marvellous alpine flowers sprinkle their spots of colour

44

around the deep blue lake where you can stop for a refreshing swim. On sunny weekends in the main season you will have to share your enjoyment with many others. A much more remote walk, but more demanding, is to go up past some more lakes to the Col de la Vallée Étroite.

From **Les Bruyères** car park, 1758m, go over the bridge and follow the yellow signs to Lac de Lou. From the signpost at 2100m above the **Refuge du Lac de Lou** go along the Sentier no. 15 across the northwest slope above the lake. Be careful – if you go along the lake shore, you should ascend on the right before the bridge at the south end of the lake, otherwise you will find it impossible to cross the torrential stream of the Ruisseau du Revers to reach the path up to the pass. Go over the Torrent du Lou, then on the level along the left hand bank of the Ruisseau du Revers. By two alpine mountain huts it starts to get steep as you continue southwestwards up to the first lake of the **Lacs de Pierre Blanche**, 2304m. The others are to be found a good way higher up, the last at an altitude of 2460m. Continue from this lake southwards to the **Col de la Vallée Étroite**, 2732m, with its fantastic views down into the Maurienne.

Either return the same way or choose to cross from the Croix du Bienheureux Paul below Lac de Lou over onto the right hand side of the valley and return via La Chasse, 1900m, to the car park at **Les Bruyères** (¼ hr. longer).

45

9 Refuge du Saut – Lac du Mont Coua, 2672m

From the verdant nature reserve into a glacial waste

Lac de Tuéda – Refuge du Saut – Lac du Mont Coua and back

Starting and finishing point: Lac de Tuéda, 1700m, large car park with info board between Méribel-Mottaret and the lake, approach from the Tarentaise along the D 90.
Walking times: Lac de Tuéda (car park) – Refuge du Saut 2 hrs., Refuge du Saut – Lac du Mont Coua 2 hrs., Lac du Mont Coua – Lac de Tuéda (car park) 3 hrs.; total time 7 hrs.
Height difference: 1000m.
Grade: no problems up to the Refuge du Saut, then a steep path, in the upper area sometimes no paths (cairns) through moraine debris, jumping over some of the streams requires some courage depending on the level of the water.

Accommodation: Refuge du Saut, July/Aug., ⓒ 06 03 85 10 39.
Alternatives: 1) From the Refuge du Saut go east across the Col de Chanrouge to the Lacs Merlet, 2 hrs. (compare Walk 10). Continue across the Col de la Platta, Col de Chanrossa and the Col du Fruit back to the Lac de Tuéda, 3 hrs. You go round the impressive massif of Aiguille du Fruit on the way. 2) From the car park you can also reach the Lac de Tuéda via the Sentier botanique, about ½ hr. longer.
Maps: IGN Top 25, sheet 3534 OT, Les Trois Vallées. Modane; or walking map Didier Richard, 1:50,000, sheet 11, Vanoise massif et parc national.

Towards the end of the 18th century the Glacier de Gébroulaz reached another 100 metres up to the Refuge du Saut. The only privatized glacier in France has retreated a long way today and left behind a fascinating landscape of moraine. In complete contrast to this is the refreshing greenery of the Plan de Tuéda nature reserve. A turquoise blue glacial stream meanders through gleaming meadows while chamois gambol on the precipitous crags of the Aiguille du Fruit and golden eagles circulate above. Around 1756 they stumbled across a vein of silver near the Refuge du Saut. Under difficult conditions, German and Piemontese helped with the mining of the treasured mineral (1758-1778) which was then transported on the backs of mules to the banks of the Isère for processing.

In the Vallon du Fruit.

From the car park go along the broad footpath to **Lac de Tuéda** or on the eastern side via the Sentier botanique onto the Plan de Tuéda and to the bridge at the head of the valley. Continue on the south side of the stream steeply up into the pretty high valley of Vallon du Fruit.

Go along a gentle path past the **Chalet de la Plagne**, 2013m, until the valley narrows to a gorge. After a short incline through the eye of the needle you reach the plain with the **Refuge du Saut**, 2126m. From the hut go right on a strenuous ascent high above the Doron des Allues, then across a side stream and continue through moraine debris towards the Glacier de Gébroulaz. Before the path gets lost in the debris go to the left across a bridge and follow the tracks to the east. Go over another stream and up along its right hand bank to a pool. On a wide bend to the left ascend steeply onto the high terrace with the **Lac du Mont Coua**, 2672m.
Return the same way.

10 Lacs Merlet, 2449m

Through a wonderful high valley to idyllic lakes

Grand Prâlin – Vallée des Avals – Refuge du Grand Plan – Lacs Merlet – Lac du Pêtre – Grand Prâlin

Starting and finishing point: Grand Prâlin, 1722m, car park at the settlement of chalets at the edge of the forest; approach from Courchevel, 1650m, first road to the left, following the signs for 'rue du Belvédère'.
Walking times: Grand Prâlin – Refuge du Grand Plan 3 hrs., Refuge du Grand Plan – Lacs Merlet, upper lake ½ hr., Lacs Merlet – Lac du Pêtre ¼ hr., Lac du Pêtre – Grand Prâlin 2¼ hrs.; total time 6 hrs.
Height difference: 750m.
Grade: mountain walk suitable for families, for the most part along broad paths.
Food and accommodation: Refuge du Grand Plan, July to Sept., ✆ 06 11 95 10 95, Refuge des Lacs Merlet, always open, unstaffed, ✆ 04 79 08 71 49.
Alternative: there or back via Mont Bel-Air and the Col de la Platta (3 hrs. from the upper lake in descent), the only problem being the signs of winter tourism marring the landscape (lift pylons etc.).
Maps: IGN Top 25, sheet 3534 OT, Les Trois Vallées. Modane; or Didier Richard walking map, 1:50,000, sheet 11, Vanoise massif et parc national.
Tip: a very beautiful start into the Vallée des Avals is the Lac de la Rosière with picnic area, botanical theme path and the Cascades des Poux. The height difference is then increased by 200m and the total time by 1 hr.

The Refuge des Lacs Merlet.

However close this mini New York of Courchevel might be and its whole lift complex, they manage to remain out of sight on this walk. A surprisingly unspoilt landscape lies hidden between rugged mountain slopes in the shadow of the winter metropolis and the charming high valley of Avals allows you an especially delightful approach into the heart of the Vanoise National Park. A favourite destination in this area is Lacs Merlet, two steel blue lakes at the foot of the Aiguille du Fruit where you can watch the splendid rainbow trout jumping. The first lake also holds the record as the deepest of all the natural lakes in the Vanoise Alps – 28m.

From the car park follow the road at the edge of the forest up to the end, then continue along a comfortable forest path into the idyllic **Vallée des**

Avals. Go up over several high ledges upstream until the drivable track forks before the Chalets de la Grande Val. Continue right and at the next signpost go to the right again. On a wide bend to the west (Mont Blanc now emerges into view) the route leads into a small hollow with the **Refuge du Grand Plan**, 2320m.

Follow the signpost just above the hut to the left. Go up a short steep incline along a mountain ridge and into the broad mountain basin with the **Lacs Merlet**, 2391m and 2449m. The rustic Finnish hut, the Refuge des Lacs Merlet, 2388m, lies on the right above.

From the fork in the paths below the hut continue along the ridge to the south, then descend across marvellous alpine meadows onto the hiking path which runs up to the Col de Chanrouge. Go along this path to the left past **Lac du Pêtre**, 2282m, back to your ascent route and return to the car park.

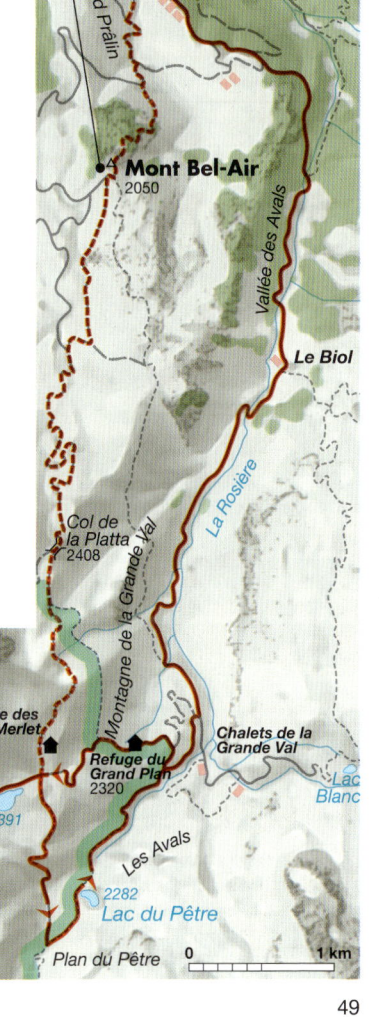

11 Petit Mont Blanc, 2677m

Peak in a lunar landscape

Grand Prâlin – Vallée des Avals – Col des Saulces – Col du Mône – Petit Mont Blanc – Col des Saulces – Combe des Roches – Grand Prâlin

Looking back into the Vallée des Avals.

Starting point: Grand Prâlin,1722m, see Walk 10.
Walking times: Grand Prâlin – Col des Saulces 3 hrs., Col des Saulces – Col du Mône – Petit Mont Blanc ½ hr., Petit Mont Blanc – Col des Saulces ½ hr., Col des Saulces – Combe des Roches 1 hr., Combe des Roches – Grand Prâlin 1½ hrs.; total time 6½ hrs.
Height difference: about 1100m.
Grade: a few exposed sections only in the summit area (steep, slippery), the descent through the Combe des Roches is also very steep.
Food and accommodation: Refuge du Grand Plan, July to Sept., ✆ 06 11 95 10 95.
Alternative: shorter, but steeper and not as lovely, are the approaches from the Pont de Gerlon at Pralognan, the Pont du Diable at Les Prioux and from Les Prioux itself.
Maps: IGN Top 25, sheet 3534 OT, Les Trois Vallées. Modane; or Didier Richard walking map, 1: 50,000, sheet 11, Vanoise massif et parc national.

It was certainly not Mont Blanc, but the glimmering white gypsum landscape of the summit that may have inspired the name. The small white mountain which appears so striking between its dark neighbours, is a totally wonderful viewpoint from where you can see the deeply indented valley of Pralognan and the Vanoise peaks.

Go as far as the fork in the paths before the **Chalets de la Grande Val** as described in Walk 10. Past the alpine mountain huts continue along the broad path to the east which runs up round long bends to the **Col des Saulces**, 2456m. From the col go to the right around the west side of Petit Mont Blanc and cross onto the **Col du Mône**, 2533m. From there go left along the south ridge to the summit of **Petit Mont Blanc**, 2677m (orientation board). Steep zigzags take you along the exposed path across the north face into the tiny valley that leads up to the **Col des Saulces**. Go left along a good hiking path back onto the pass. Continue northwards through the valley basin below the western precipices of Rochers de Plassa. Keep left at a fork in the path and descend the **Combe des Roches**, 2193m, through a series of dramatic small valleys and hollows into the **Vallée des Avals**, where you meet your ascent route again at **Le Biol**. Turn right to go back to the starting point.

12 Crête du Mont Charvet – Col de la Grande Pierre, 2403m

A bizarre ridge full of dolines

Le Plan – Col du Golet – Crête du Mont Charvet – Col de la Grande Pierre – Le Plan

Starting point: Le Plan, 1417m, at the entrance to Pralognan take the first road to the right, a few metres to the bus stop at the edge of the forest, spring with drinking water. Approach from the Tarentaise on the D 915. Bus connection with Moûtiers (station).
Walking times: Le Plan – Col du Golet 2 hrs., Col du Golet – Crête du Mont Charvet – Col de la Grande Pierre 2 hrs., Col de la Grande Pierre – Le Plan 1¼ hrs.; total time 5¼ hrs.
Height difference: 1000m.

Grade: path between the funnel-shaped dolines at times very narrow and exposed, sure-footedness essential, steep ascent and descent.
Food: none.
Accommodation: hotels in Pralognan.
Alternative: you can also climb up to the alpine mountain huts of Lanchetton in a direct line from the small village of La Croix, ½ hr. shorter.
Map: IGN Top 25, sheet 3534 OT, Les Trois Vallées. Modane.

The mountain village of Pralognan has innumerable delightful walking routes to offer, but none of them display the fascinating natural phenomenon of a karst landscape that can be found on the Crête du Mont Charvet. The path often balances along a knife edge between the countless funnel-shaped dolines giving you the goose bumps. The view of the rock bastion above Pralognan is breathtaking, and only the view on the other side of the ridge of the resort of Courchevel could perhaps spoil this stunning sight.

Choose the forest path at the bus stop and the well. Shortly afterwards a footpath turns off from the forest road and runs northwestwards uphill, marked yellow, to the **Belvédère** (1839m, small clearing with a bench). At the fork afterwards cross to the right northwards, past the alpine mountain huts of Lanchetton and Le Laitet and across the meadows with beautiful

52

The path over the Crête du Mont Charvet goes through a fascinating karst landscape.

views onto the **Col du Golet**, 2079m. A short detour leads to the right onto the **Rocher de Villeneuve**, 2197m. Otherwise go to the left up a short incline onto the **Crête du Mont Charvet**, 2361m, a ridge covered in dolines. Keep on the ridge going south to the **Col de la Grande Pierre**, 2403m. From the pass descend to the left very steeply down through the Couloir de la Grande Pierre to the mountain pasture of **La Montagne**, 2006m. Go right along the drivable track until a blue marked path leads to the left steeply down through the forest and meets the ascent route again just above the Belvédère.

13 Les Cirques de Pralognan

Magnificent rock basin, dramatic waterfalls, glacial slopes

Les Prioux – Chalet des Nants – Col de la Vallette – Cirque du Petit Marchet – Col du Grand Marchet – Cirque de l'Arcelin – Les Prioux

Starting point: Les Prioux, 1711m, in the valley of the Doron de Chavière, 4km from Pralognan. Approach from the Tarentaise along the D 915.
Walking times: Les Prioux – Chalet des Nants 1½ hrs., Chalet des Nants – Col de la Vallette 1¼ hrs., Col de la Vallette – Cirque du Petit Marchet ½ hr., Cirque du Petit Marchet – Col du Grand Marchet 1½ hrs., Col du Grand Marchet – Cirque de l'Arcelin 1 hr., Cirque de l'Arcelin – Les Prioux 1¾ hrs.; total time 7½ hrs.
Height difference: 1400m.
Grade: very long mountain walk on narrow paths with a few steep ascents. The descent is a bit tricky from the Col du Grand Marchet: exposed and slippery, sometimes made safe with chains; sure-footedness and a head for heights essential.
Food and accommodation: Refuge Le Repoju in Les Prioux, ✆ 04 79 08 73 79; Refuge de la Vallette, 14.6.-14.9., ✆ 04 79 22 96 38.
Alternative: start from the last car park in the valley of Doron Chavière. Ascent via Montaimont and Plan des Bôs. The high mountain trail meets the described route at the Chalet des Nants. An additional 2½ hrs.
Map: IGN Top 25, sheet 3534 OT, Les Trois Vallées. Modane.

In an idyllic location – the 'mountaineer's village' of Pralognan.

Steep gully into the Cirque du Dard.

Nature has created a huge mountain landscape here. Below the glacial plateau of the Glaciers de la Vanoise you will find imposing rock bastions, towers and serrated peaks. In between there are breathtaking rocky valley basins where foaming waterfalls cascade down from the steep rock faces and tiny turquoise coloured streams meander through luxuriant green meadows. Amongst the constantly changing views of this mountainous region the first sight of the vertical precipices of Roc de la Vallette is spectacular on the ascent to the Col de la Vallette, then from the pass, of the glaciated summit of Grande Casse. In complete contrast to this is the return through the unspoilt fairytale forest of Forêt d'Isertan, then later in the val-

You reach the Cirque de l'Arcelin along a path protected with chains.

ley the dramatic Doron de Chavière in whose clear pool you can take a delightfully invigorating dip.

From the main road just after **Les Prioux**, 1711m, follow the hiking path to the left and into the mountain through bushes. Go left at a fork in the path. Go across two bridges, past the ruin of the **Chalet des Nants**, 2184m, and climb steeply up at the left edge of the Cirque des Nants, then cross to the north and onto the **Col de la Vallette**, 2554m. The pretty Finnish houses of the Refuge de la Vallette lie on the right above. Continue along the high trail into the **Cirque du Petit Marchet** (2392m). You can also go round this on the regular hiking path to the left, but that would be a pity. A path, marked with cairns, leads from the rocky valley basin on the east side around the steep slopes of Petit Marchet and meets the regular hiking path again in the **Cirque du Grand Marchet** (2205m). Go to the right up a steep incline to the **Col du Grand Marchet** (2490m).

From the pass it's a slippery descent down a steep gully into the Cirque du Dard, then secured with chains across broken rocks to the fork in the **Cirque de l'Arcelin** (1881m). Go down to the left onto the roadway, past a reservoir and left again onto a high trail. With pretty views of Pralognan and the Cascade Fraîche (the waterfall can be discovered more closely along a pleasing via ferrata) you pass an opening to a tunnel, ignore the path turning off left and descend a short way to the fork above the campsite. Go left onto the Sentier Nanette which winds its way through a wild coniferous forest and then runs down onto the GR 55. Take this path to the left along the Doron de Chavière as far as the **Pont de Gerlon**, 1592m. Return along the other shore to **Les Prioux**.

14 Refuge de Péclet Polset, 2459m – Lac Blanc, 2429m

A heavenly lake in an area with ibex

Pont de la Pêche – Refuge de Péclet Polset – Lac Blanc – Chalet de Rosoire – Ritort – Pont de la Pêche

Starting point: Pont de la Pêche, 1764m, the furthest car park in the valley of Doron de Chavière, 5km from Pralognan.
Walking times: Pont de la Pêche – Refuge de Péclet Polset 2½ hrs.; Refuge de Péclet Polset – Lac Blanc ¼ hr., Lac Blanc – Refuge de Péclet Polset – Chalet de Rosoire 2¼ hrs., Chalet de Rosoire – Pont de la Pêche 1 hr.; total time 6 hrs.
Height difference: 900m, or if the ascent route is the same as the descent: 700m.

Grade: walk suitable for families if the ascent is the same as the descent route (with small children it's also a nice and simple walk as far as Alp Ritort). The return is extensively unmarked and demands a sense of direction and sure-footedness.
Food: Alpage Ritort, 1971m, refreshments and sale of cheese; Refuge du Roc de la Pêche and Refuge de Péclet Polset.
Accommodation: Refuge du Roc de la Pêche, with Jacuzzi, Sauna, Hamam, ℂ 04 79 08 79 75, Refuge de Péclet Polset, 15.6. to 15.9., ℂ 04 79 08 72 13.
Map: IGN Top 25, sheet 3534 OT, Les Trois Vallées. Modane.
Tips: continuation of the GR 55 over the Col de Chavière, 2796m, to the Refuge de l'Orgère. Continue along the GR 5 to the Refuge du Fond d'Aussois and over the Col d'Aussois, 2916m, back to the starting point: 2-3 days. Or from Lac Blanc over the Col du Souffre (2819m, only with high alpine experience) to the Refuge du Saut, back over Col Rouge, 2731m, to the starting point: 2-3 days.

The GR 55 is a section of the popular long distance hiking trail around the Vanoise glacier. On sunny weekends in July and August it's often quite busy with day-trippers on the trail between the pretty destinations of the Refuge du Roc de la Pêche and the Alpage de Ritort. But this reduces very quickly the further you go into the valley. You ascend the valley from the verdant greenery into a rugged mountain landscape. Near to the modern Refuge de Péclet Polset you will come across a particular gem, Lac Blanc. Its shape is fascinating – with its large curved shorelines the glacial lake nestles into a rock bowl. Depending on the time of year its colour changes from a rich turquoise to an emerald green, embraced by the soft green of the shoreline meadows and draped by the sheer rock faces where a colony of ibex lives.

Lake below the western face of Pointe de l'Observatoire.

Watching ibex at Lac Blanc.

From the car park go along the GR 55 upstream on the broad gravel path to the right over the bridge, **Pont de la Pêche**, 1764m, and over a first high ledge to the **Refuge du Roc de la Pêche**, 1911m. Continue following the broad path southwards which runs almost interminably into the head of the valley and up to the **Refuge de Péclet Polset**, 2459m. On the right past the refuge go northwestwards to the nearby **Lac Blanc**, 2429m.

From the **Refuge de Péclet Polset** take the track for a short way back to the big left hand bend. Go right there onto a path which leads towards the moraine that comes down from the Brèche de la Coix de la Rue. Before reaching the moraine turn off the path left, go across the stream and round a wide bend without paths northwards onto a grassy ridge, 2507m, below the west flank of Pointe de l'Observatoire. If you climb up a little further over the boulder fields to the east, you meet a marvellously remote lake which invites you to stop for a swim and a picnic. Continue along some tracks which are not easy to find between the boulders to point 2444. Cross the pastures above the Chalet des Planettes onto the **Col des Planettes**, 2448m. The path is clearer again here. Zigzag down to the **Chalet de Rosoire**, 2208m. After the alpine mountain hut you meet the hiking path that comes from the Col d'Aussois. Go left down a steep descent to the **Alpage de Ritort**, 1971m, where the route meets the GR 55 again. Turn right to return to the **Pont de la Pêche**.

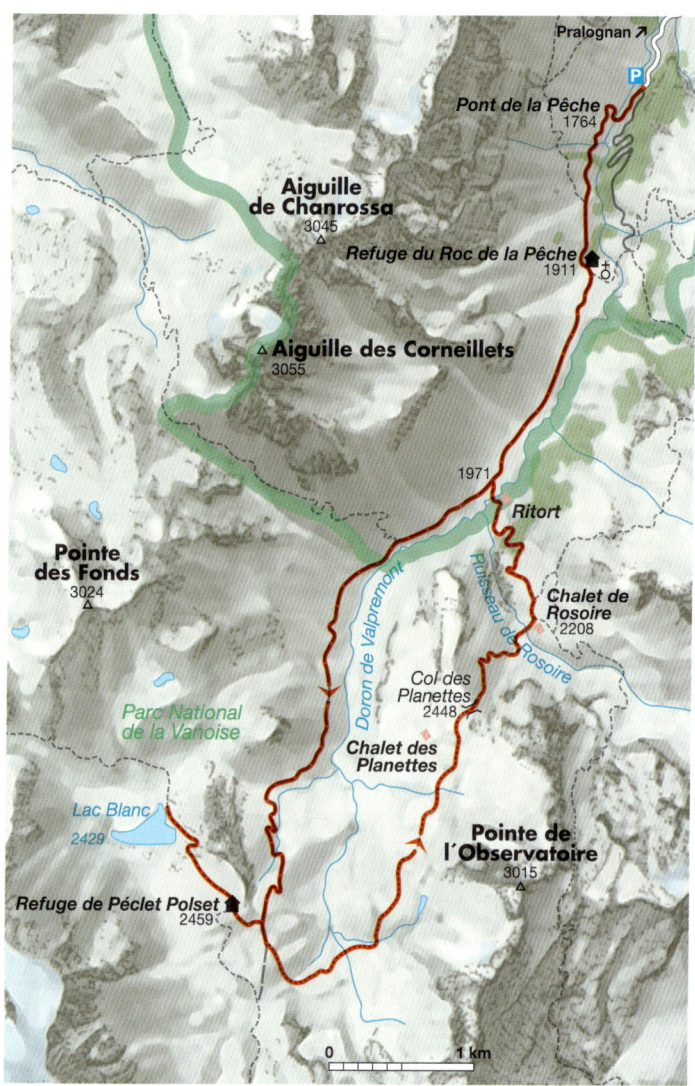

15 Tour de l'Aiguille des Aimes

Dramatic glacial scenery and three passes with wonderful views

Le Laisonnay – Refuge de la Glière – Col de la Croix des Frêtes – Col du Palet – Col de la Grassaz – Le Laisonnay

Starting and finishing point: Le Laisonnay d'en haut, 1579m, at the head of the valley, 8km from Champagny-le-Haut.
Walking times: Le Laisonnay d'en haut – Refuge de la Glière a good 1¼ hrs., Refuge de la Glière – Col de la Croix des Frêtes 1½ hrs., Col de la Croix des Frêtes – Col de la Grassaz just under 1¼ hrs., Col de la Grassaz – Refuge de la Glière 1¼ hrs., Refuge de la Glière – Le Laisonnay ¾ hr.; total time 6 hrs.
Height difference: 1250m.
Grade: a few steep ascents; patches of old snow in the area of the pass in June.
Food and accommodation: Refuge du Laisonnay, staffed May to Sept., ✆ 06 08 54 34 61, ✆ 04 79 24 31 24; Refuge de la Glière, staffed July/Aug., ✆ 04 79 55 02 64; Refuge du Col du Palet, staffed 15.6.-15.9., ✆ 04 79 07 91 47 or ✆ 06 76 84 47 91.
Alternative: the walk can be extended via the Col du Plan Séry and the Refuge de Plaisance back to Le Laisonnay (spectacular, but an additional 2 hrs.).
Maps: IGN Top 25 sheet 3534 OT Les Trois Vallées. Modane and sheet 3633 ET Tignes. Val d'Isère or Didier Richard walking map, 1: 50,000, sheet 11, Vanoise massif et parc national.
Tips: from the Col du Palet you can walk east to Tigne and Val d'Isère (see Walks 22, 23, 24) or northwards to the Porte de Rosuel (see Walk 17). If you only want a short walk, you will enjoy the themed guided walk of the 'sentier découverte' Le Bois – Friburge – Le Laisonnay, 1½ hrs. each way.

Above the rocky valley basin of Glière.

Refuge du Laisonnay with the Cascade du Py.

While tourism is throbbing away in the nearby Trois Vallées during the winter season and leaves behind lifeless resorts in summer, the upper Champagny valley has remained refreshingly unspoilt. Low-key tourism is written large here. Ancient hamlets, tiny chapels and wonderful picnic spots are tucked away into luxuriant meadows in the bottom of valleys. You can wander along enchanting footpaths through a small paradise, marvel at the imposing steep rock faces and the thundering waterfall of the Cascade du Py right at the back of the valley by the pretty Refuge du Laisonnay. It's especially spectacular if you hike up into the rocky valley basin of Glière where impressive massifs with rugged glacial slopes loom above – the north face of Grande Casse with the Glacier de l'Epéna in the centre point. A walk around the massif of Aiguille des Aimes adds to your enjoyment of the view and affords you glimpses into Val d'Isère and the Vallon de Rosuel.

From the furthest car park at **Le Laisonnay d'en haut**, 1579m, follow the roadway to the left going southeastwards. This runs high above the right hand bank of the Doron de Champagny to the **Refuge de la Glière**, 1996m. Continue along the hiking trail, always taking shortcuts from the roadway where possible, and ascend the southern hillside and along a high ledge eastwards. Go past the Chalet du Plan du Sél to the left hand bend with a fork. Turn right into the little high valley with **Lac du Grand Plan**, 2480m, and go northeastwards to the **Col de la Croix des Frêtes**, 2647m. Cross right onto the nearby **Col du Palet**, 2652m, where the route meets the white and red marked GR 5. Descend the GR 5 to the north and leave the Refuge du Col du Palet on the right. At **Lac du Gratteleu**, 2512m, an unmarked path turns off left which leads round a wide left hand bend to your ascent path to the **Col de la Grassaz**, 2637m.

From the Col de la Grassaz go southwards across sloping meadows to the roadway of the ascent route and via the **Refuge de la Glière** back to the starting point.

64

16 Pointe de la Vélière, 2467m

Belvedere above the Vallée de Champagny

Champagny-le-Haut – La Vélière – Col de la Bauche de Mio – Pointe de la Vélière – Col de la Bauche de Mio – Le Tougne – Plan du Bouc – Champagny-le-Haut

Starting point: Champagny-le-Haut/Le Bois, 1470m, car park at the Refuge du Bois.
Walking times: Champagny-le-Haut – La Vélière 1¼ hrs., La Vélière – Col de la Bauche de Mio 1¼ hrs., Col de la Bauche de Mio – Pointe de la Vélière ½ hr., Pointe de la Vélière – Le Tougne a good ¼ hr., Le Tougne – Champagny-le-Haut just under 1¼ hrs.; total time 4½ hrs.
Height difference: 1040m.
Grade: only a short section of the descent from the Plan du Bouc is really exposed and demands sure-footedness. Be careful when wet.
Accommodation: Chalet-Refuge du Bois, ✆/fax: 04 79 55 05 79; Camping Le Canada, ✆ 04 79 55 03 80.
Alternative: a fantastic viewing summit with a view of Mont Blanc is Roche de Mio, 2739m. The following route is recommended for fit adventurous climbers: Champagny-le-Haut – Le Tovet – La Chiaupe 2¼ hrs., La Chiaupe – Col de Frête – Roche de Mio 1½ hrs., Roche de Mio – Pointe du Tougne – Col de la Bauche de Mio – Pointe de la Vélière 1¼ hrs., Pointe de la Vélière – Le Tougne – Plan du Bouc – Champagny-le-Haut

1½ hrs.; total time 6½ hrs., height difference about 1270m. The section from Roche de Mio over the Pointe du Tougne to the Col de la Bauche de Mio is without paths and needs fine weather, a good sense of direction and sure-footedness (graded 'black').
Map: IGN Top 25, sheet 3532 ET, Les Arcs. La Plagne.
Tip: the via ferrata du Plan du Bouc promises the pleasure of exposure with extensive views. Info board and car park at the chapel of Notre-Dame de la Compassion at the entrance to the valley.

Your attention is immediately drawn to the white cross of the Pointe de la Vélière if you wander through the lovely high valley of Champagny and the thought of standing on the top is then planted in your mind. In fact the walk promises a fantastic round walk across remote alpine pastures and from the ridge of Pointe de la Vélière, a spectacular view into the valley.

Go past the **Refuge du Bois** into the village and go left through Le Bois dessous out of the village again. After the bridge turn right onto the field path which ascends steeply westwards up the southern hillside. Then on a sharp right hand bend go round a rock barrier into the narrow furrow of the valley of the Gurre de la Chiserette Rau. Keep left at the fork and continue to the alpine mountain hut of **La Vélière**, 2162m. Take the wide bend to the west through the head of the valley and onto the **Col de la Bauche de Mio**, 2502m. Now go left along some tracks with views along the ridge to the summit cross of **Pointe de la Vélière**, 2467m, visible from a long way off. You can take a shortcut without paths and requiring sure-footedness, directly across the steep pastures. Continue westwards to the ruins of le Tougne, or otherwise go back along the ridge all the way to the pass and descend left to the crossroads where you keep left again. Go via **Le Tougne**, 2138m, to the fork in the paths at the stream and continue left along the grassy path which then runs close to the forest boundary eastwards to the **Plan du Bouc**,1952m. Now exposed on a narrow path, go above the rocks with the via ferrata to the wobbly suspension bridge with a waterfall. The little path joins the broad ascent path just afterwards.

67

17 Mont Jovet, 2558m

The green mountain with a breathtaking panorama

Parking de la Plate Form – Chalet de la Côte – Refuge du Mont Jovet – Mont Jovet – Halle de Fruit Commun – Parking de la Plate Form

Starting point: Parking de la Plate Form, 1821m, just before the end of the tarmac of the winding mountain road, 6km above Notre-Dame du Pré. Approach from Moûtiers along the N 90 in the direction of Bourg St-Maurice, Les Plaines turn-off.
Walking times: car park – Chalet de la Côte ¾ hr., Chalet de la Côte – Refuge du Mont Jovet 1¼ hrs., Refuge du Mont Jovet – Mont Jovet ½ hr., Mont Jovet – Halle de Fruit Commun 1¼ hrs., Halle de Fruit Commun – car park ¼ hr.; total time 4 hrs.
Height difference: 820m.
Grade: mostly good paths. A certain amount of sure-footedness required for the summit area.
Food: Refuge du Mont Jovet; Restaurant la Frutière with small village shop (closed on Wednesday) in Notre-Dame du Pré.
Accommodation: Refuge du Mont Jovet, CAF, ✆ 04 79 08 11 20; Gîte rural in Notre-Dame du Pré.
Alternative: you can also walk up from the Bozel valley. Approach from Bozel to Villemartin, then 4km to the hamlet of la Cour, car park 800m after the end of the tarmac road. Ascent 2½ hrs.
Map: IGN Top 25, sheet 3532 OT Massif du Beaufortain. Moûtiers. La Plagne.

Despite its relatively low height, Mont Jovet delivers quite a remarkable view. As soon as you come out of the forest, a few minutes after the car park, the view opens out over lovely alpine pastures and a row of peaks between

Alpine roses at the Chalet de la Côte.

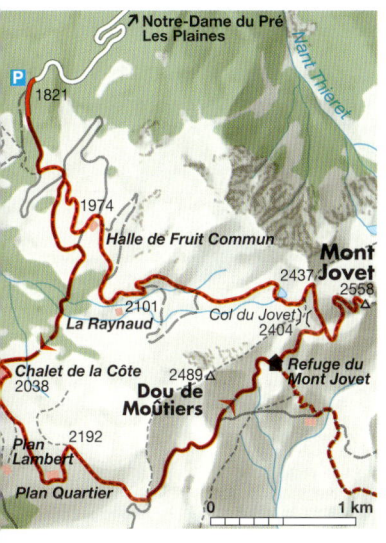

the deeply indented valleys of the Tarentaise. Mont Blanc draws your attention in the north, but then disappears as you walk round the grass covered massif. In return you are afforded a clear view of the famous Les Trois Vallées skiing area and the glacier-covered Vanoise massif. Once you have reached the top of Mont Jovet, you are greeted with a sea of rugged peaks where you can stand and gaze ... and Mont Blanc pops up again, if it's not hiding behind its usual midday shroud.

From the car park, 1821m, follow the road out of the forest which soon turns into a gravel path. Take a shortcut across the first long bend, then continue right along the roadway to the **Chalet de la Côte**, 2038m. At the signposts above the ruins of the building turn to the right. Carry on across the southwestern sloping meadows of Montagne de la Côte to the alpine mountain hut of Plan Quartier. On a wide bend to the left continue as far as point 2192 where you meet a cross path. Turn right here and you come to a roadway which, with beautiful views, winds up left to the **Refuge du Mont Jovet**. After the refuge go on the right across verdant meadows then steeply ascend across the western hillside towards the ridge and the summit of **Mont Jovet**, 2558m, with an orientation board.

Descend the west ridge into the hollow, 2437m. There descend westwards to a pool. Continue across meadows and the furrows of streams, then along a gravel track past **La Raynaud** alpine mountain hut, 2101m. Go round a wide bend to the north down to the **Halle de Fruit Commun**, 1974m. A path takes a shortcut across the wide bends of the track which eventually leads you back to the car park.

Refuge du Mont Jovet.

18 Porte de Rosuel – Lac de la Plagne, 2145m

A picturesque end of the valley

Rosuel – Lac de la Plagne – Refuge Entre le Lac – Chalets de la Plagne – Perte du Ponturin – Rosuel

Starting point: Porte de Rosuel, 1556m, with a large car park. Approach from the Tarentaise: turn off from the N 90 between Aime and Bourg-St-Maurice onto the D 87, past Peisey-Nancroix and continue up the valley to the end of the road.
Walking times: Rosuel – Refuge Entre le Lac 2¾ hrs., Refuge Entre le Lac – GR 5 1 hr., GR 5 – Perte du Ponturin 1 hr., Perte du Ponturin – Rosuel 1 hr.; total time 5¾ hrs.
Height difference: about 800m.
Grade: not a difficult mountain walk, but with a steep incline at the start. The only exposed section is the crossing of the scree slope above the valley basin of Lac de la Plagne.
Food and accommodation: Refuge de Rosuel, staffed 8.6. – 14.9., ✆ 04 79 07 94 03; Refuge Entre le Lac, staffed middle of June to middle of Sept., ✆ 04 79 04 20 44;
Refuge du Mont Pourri, staffed 14.6. – 4.9., ✆ 04 79 07 90 43.
Alternatives: 1) Fabulous extension of the walk along a high trail to the Refuge du Mont Pourri. Descent via the Chalets des Loyes and through the Combe du Barmail to the hamlet of Beaupraz and back to the Port de Rosuel; from the turn-off at point 2092 3 hrs.
2) From the Refuge Entre le Lac a delightful walk over the Col du Plan Séry (1¾ hrs.) into the high valley of Champagny. Return via Walk 15.
Map: IGN Top 25, sheet 3532 ET, Les Arcs. La Plagne.
Tip: the exciting via ferrata des Bettières with a short approach (info board at the car park) and view of the picturesque valley basin: Refuge de Rosuel – start of via ferrata ¼ hr., via ferrata 2 hrs., descent 1 hr.; total time 3¼ hrs.

Gateway to the Vanoise National Park – Porte de Rosuel.

Waterfall in the Vallon de Rosuel.

The Vallon de Rosuel is one of the most impressive gateways into the Vanoise National Park. Vertical rock walls create an impressive spectacle while waterfalls cascade down the sheer slopes, fed by the glaciers of the huge west face of Mont Pourri and Dôme de la Sache. Old wooden chalets lie scattered across the verdant valley floor. The Refuge de Rosuel, although modern, is harmoniously integrated and makes quite an impression with its fancy wooden construction and roof covered in turf. Due to a high ledge you cannot see the continuation of the valley. Continue along the GR 5 into the rugged landscape of the fold in the mountain until you finally reach Lac de la Plagne which is tucked into the head of the valley.

At the fork in the path after the **Refuge de Rosuel**, 1556m, follow the white and red marked GR 5 to the right. The stony path runs up the hillside with a marvellous view of spraying waterfalls towards the gorge-like, wooded valley narrowing. After the larch wood go through the open high valley keeping to the left hand bank of the Ponturin stream up a moderate incline to the **Lac de la Plagne**, 2145m. Just a little to the southwest behind it you come directly to the **Refuge Entre le Lac**.

The following suggestion is a more varied return route which involves, however, another short ascent: behind the refuge follow the path in the direction of the Col du Plan Séry until, about 30 minutes later at point 2320, a path branches off to the left. At first head towards a band of rock, then traverse across the steep scree slopes of Aiguille de Bacque, continuing high above the valley basin eastwards until you meet the GR 5. Follow this to the left, now along the other side of the valley, over green pastures and gurgling streams and gently descend to the **Chalets de la Plagne**. At the fork beyond go left (right takes you in 1½ hrs. to the Refuge du Mont Pourri) down to the bridge and fork at **Perte du Ponturin**, 2068m. Return down the ascent path to the starting point.

In complete harmony with the landscape – the Refuge de Rosuel.

19 Lancebranlette, 2936m

Easy summit ascent with unique panorama

Hospice du Petit St-Bernard – Lancebranlette – Hospice du Petit St-Bernard

Starting point: Hospiz, 2153m, a little below the Col du Petit St-Bernard, 2188m, pass and watershed between the Tarentaise and the Aosta valley. Approach from Bourg-St-Maurice along the N 90.
Walking times: Hospiz – turn-off to lake 1½ hrs., turn-off to lake – Lancebranlette 1 hr., descent 1½ hrs.; total time 4 hrs.
Height difference: 783m.
Grade: easy mountain walk, tricky passage across the southern hillside (very steep, slippery scree slopes), not advisable when wet. Unmarked, but obvious path.
Food: Bar de Lancebranlette (very cosy) on the French side of the pass, several restaurants/bars on the Italian side.
Accommodation: Ristorante San Bernardo on the pass on the Italian side, ✆/fax 0039 01 65 84 14 44 or 033 56 37 43 13.

Alternative: worthwhile detour half way along to the Lac sans Fond, 2456m, ½ hr.
Map: IGN Top 25, sheet 3531 ET, St-Gervais.

Already in Roman times, the Col du Petit St-Bernard was one of the most important crossings between France and Italy. Today the Mont Blanc tunnel takes the main traffic away and the pass is left to the tourists. The main attractions are a theme path (sentier de découverte), a botanical garden (jardin botanique de la Chanousia), hiking trails or simply enjoying the view. But this is nothing compared to the panorama which awaits you on the summit of Lancebranlette. The close view of Mont Blanc is especially impressive, but also the Matterhorn, Monte Rosa and Weisshorn are recognizable amongst the northeastern array of peaks. The Mont Pourri dominates the Vanoise massif in the south. The pass owes its name to Saint Bernhard of Aosta who, just as he did on the Grand St. Bernhard, founded a hospice in the 11th century here which is a favourite starting point today for the walk onto Lancebranlette.

From the **Hospice** take the path to the north, past a small lake, over the stream and zigzag up the pastures in a westerly direction. You come to a ridge which you follow steadily uphill. Leave the turn-off to the Lac sans Fond on the left and continue to point 2700. The path leaves the ridge here and runs on the right of it across an unpleasantly slippery scree slope onto

the broad southern hillside. Continue up round zigzags to the summit of **Lancebranlette**, 2936m. Just below the summit there's a bench seat and an orientation board.
Return the same way.

A walk for connoisseurs with a view of Mont Blanc.

20 Lac du Retour, 2397m

Picturesque lakeland terraces in sight of Mont Pourri

Le Châtelard – Le Vaz – Kar Nant du Piche – Passage du Retour – Lac du Retour – Plan Pigeux – Le Vaz – Le Châtelard

Starting point: Le Châtelard, 1500m, pretty mountain village above the D 902 in Val d'Isère, turn-off from the pass to the Col du Petit St-Bernard between Bourg St-Maurice and La Rosière.
Walking times: Le Châtelard – Kar Nant du Piche 1¼ hrs., Kar Nant du Piche – Lac du Retour 1½ hrs., Lac du Retour – Plan Pigeux ¾ hr., Plan Pigeux – Le Châtelard 1 hr.; total time 4½ hrs.
Height difference: about 1000m.
Grade: rather more demanding mountain walk which requires a sense of direction on the path up that is only marked with cairns. A steep slope in descent where sure-footedness is important.
If you do not feel confident on the unmarked path, you can take the red marked path to the Lac du Retour for the ascent as well as the descent.
Food: none.
Alternative: possible to descend from the Col du Retour to La Savonne (1½ hrs.), and/or to the Refuge du Ruitor (2 hrs.) (marked red), ideal link with Walk 21.
Map: IGN Top 25, sheet 3532 ET, Les Arcs, La Plagne.
Tip: Chambre d'hôtes de Montperron, charming location above Séez, ✆ 04 79 40 18 29.

The ascent leads through an unspoilt landscape where you will hardly meet a soul because you are not walking along regular hiking trails. This increases the chance of coming across some animals. Dramatically beautiful terraces with high moorland and small pools, alpine roses and bilberries are

On the way up to Lac du Retour with a view of Mont Pourri.

a feast for the eyes. The view of Mont Pourri is at its most beautiful when you see it reflected in the Lac du Retour.

Go through the small village of **Le Châtelard**, 1500m, and walk along the roadway eastwards on the level to the group of houses of **Le Vaz**, 1515m, with an idyllic picnic spot and drinking well. At the edge of the forest ascend left along the broad path. After passing the channel of the Nant du Piche stream, an unmarked path branches off at point 1723 to the right and runs parallel to the slope in a southerly direction. Just before the furrow of the stream go left up along some feint tracks through bushes. Cairns help you find your way. You reach the hidden high valley of **Nant du Piche**, with a marvellous view of the tiny church of Le Châtelard. Continue along the left hand bank of the stream into the wide hollow of a cirque. Keeping right, follow the cairns and ascend diagonally southwards to a cross path and go along it to the left. After crossing a slope you reach a small high plateau with a small lake. Take the tracks going west to the next terrace, with a fabulous view of Mont Pourri. Ascend northwards along the left hand bank of the steep channel of the stream, then turn to the northwest. Go across a plateau and towards the elongated grassy ridge past some more lakes. If you follow the line of the ridge to the north you will meet the red marked path which, to the right, soon takes you onto the plateau with good views and **Lac du Retour**, 2397m, lying on the right in a hollow. Go along the red marked path to the west back over the small col, the Passage du Retour. On a steep zigzag path descend a slippery couloir and round a right hand bend to the ruins of **Plan Pigeux**, 1958m. Here, take the path to the left, through luxuriant green meadows down the valley towards the forest and back via Le Vaz to **Le Châtelard**.

21 Tour du Montséti

Varied circular walk through a hidden mountain paradise

La Savonne – Refuge du Ruitor – Col de Montséti – Lac Noir – Refuge de l'Archeboc – La Savonne

The Refuge de l'Archeboc in the Vallon de Mercuel.

Starting point: La Savonne, 1771m, car park at the 'Usine électrique' just before the group of houses. Approach from Val d'Isère, turn-off from Ste-Foy-Tarentaise.
Walking times: La Savonne – Refuge du Ruitor ½ hr., Refuge du Ruitor – Lac Noir 2 hrs., Lac Noir – Refuge de l'Archeboc 1 hr., Refuge de l'Archeboc – La Savonne 1½ hrs.; total time 5 hrs.
Height difference: 800m.
Grade: not a difficult walk, but with a few steep sections, also good to do with children who like walking.
Food and accommodation: Refuge du Ruitor, self-catering hut, key with the Mercier family in La Masure, ✆ 04 79 06 92 12; Refuge de l'Archeboc, 15. June to 15. Sept., ✆ 04 79 06 87 19, long evening sunshine, climbing wall at the house.
Map: IGN Top 25, sheet 3532 ET, Les Arcs. La Plagne.
Tips: a fantastic walk also in the opposite direction. This route can be linked via the Sentier des Refuges with Walk 20 (Chapelle St-Pierre – Col du Retour 2 hrs.) and/or Walk 22 (Refuge de l'Archeboc – Gîte d'Etape de Chenal 5½ hrs.) into a multi-day trek. Otherwise it's a wonderful area for ski tours! The Refuge de l'Archeboc is open in winter at weekends on request.

A walk round the Arête de Montséti affords you views into the two very attractive high valleys. The idyllic high valley of Sassière opens out at the Chapelle St-Pierre. The Ruisseau du Grand meanders through an abundance of blossoming flowers. In the alpine spring you will be enchanted by the enumerable orchids and the hillside is totally covered with alpine roses.

The border ridge with Italy towers up at the head of the valley: Grand and Petit Assaly, Noeud des Vedettes and Becca du Lac, and below them the white tongue of the Glacier de l'Invernet. The Vallon de Mercuel appears rather more bleak, but on closer inspection, it is also filled with wonderful flowers. The border ridge is now dominated by Pointe d'Archeboc in the southeast. The crossing of the pass between the two valleys is accompanied by many idyllic small lakes and superb views.

Just before the group of houses at **La Savonne**, 1771m, a path ascends up left to take a shortcut from the roadway into the high valley of La Sassière. Look back for a fabulous view of Mont Pourri. From point 1934 continue along the roadway. At the **Chapelle St-Pierre** go left and through the high valley of Sassière. Just behind the **Refuge du Ruitor**, 2032m, turn right over the stream to the ruin of La Sassière. Go over another small stream and up the slope covered with alpine rose on the zigzag path. You soon reach a marvellous high plateau full of small lakes. Keeping right, continue southwards following the cairns and up a steep incline onto the **Col de Montséti**, 2571m. After the pass there's a short descent in a southeasterly direction to **Lac Noir**, 2483m. Carry on along the marked path southeastwards from its western end to a small lake, then go steeply down across meadows into the Vallon de Mercuel with the **Refuge de l'Archeboc**, 2029m. Take the roadway to the right as far as the alpine mountain huts of Les Côtes where the hiking path turns off right. This beautiful path runs in a gentle up-and-down through a light coniferous wood, parallel to the western slopes of the Arête de Montséti, and back to the hamlet of **La Savonne**.

22 Col du Lac Noir, 2869m – Col du Rocher Blanc, 2833m

Adventurous walk over the pass and around the border ridge with Italy

Chenal – Monal – Les Balmes – Lac Noir – Col du Lac Noir – Col du Rocher Blanc – Les Balmes – Monal – Chenal

Starting and finishing point: Chenal, 1700m, car park at the Gîte d'Étape. Approach from Bourg-St-Maurice along the D 902 in the direction of Val d'Isère. Turn off before the tunnel at Les Pigettes to the left via Le Franier to the end of the road which is open to private vehicles.
Walking times: Chenal – Monal 1 hr., Monal – Les Balmes 1½ hrs., Les Balmes – Lac Noir 1 hr., Lac Noir – Col du Lac Noir 1½ hrs., Col du Lac Noir – Col du Rocher Blanc 1 hr., Col du Rocher Blanc – Les Balmes 1½ hrs., Les Balmes – Chenal 1 hr.; total time 8½ hrs.
Height difference: about 1250m.
Grade: an ideal family walk up to the Lac Noir, but then the crossing of the pass is only for adventurous and experienced mountain walkers. The alpine terrain demands a good level of fitness, a sense of direction and sure-footedness. Some small patches of old snow are present all year round. An exposed passage (easy climbing) on the rocky ridge that divides the two passes.
Food: Gîte d'Etape de Chenal.
Accommodation: Gîte d'Etape de Chenal, ✆ 04 79 06 93 63 or 04 79 06 92 09; Gîte d'Etape de Monal, ✆ 06 07 38 24 69.
Alternative: an easy walk goes from the small weir above Le Monal to Lac du Clou, 2373m, 1 hr.
Map: IGN Top 25, sheet 3532 ET, Les Arcs. La Plagne.

After Monal, an absolutely delightful high plateau, follows the ascent through a totally forgotten high valley. It's the barrenness which makes the Vallon du Clou so enchanting.

From Pointe des Plates des Chamois glacial tongues broken into chaotic seracs roll down towards high walls of moraine. There's an impressive view of Mont Pourri in the west. Waterfalls spray out from the rock faces at Lac Noir and you can take a refreshing, but ice-cold swim in its clear blue waters. The crossing of the two passes then becomes a geology lesson for the touching. Rocks in every possible hue and colour as far as the eye can reach.

From the **Gîte d'Etape de Chenal** follow the tarmac road into the mountains and leave the road to Châtelard on the right. You pass by the hamlet of **Chenal d'en Haut**, 1743m. At a sharp right hand bend go straight ahead onto the roadway. After the group of houses of **Combaz** go right and through a small gorge onto the high plateau of **Monal**, 1874m. Go through the hamlet and turn right to the edge of the forest where a path branches off left, ascends steeply through the forest and meets a drivable track that you follow left into the Vallon de Clou. Continue along the left hand bank across the flat valley floor, then ascending past two chalets of **Les Balmes**, continue eastwards through the now narrow gorge-like high valley into the small rocky basin of **Lac Noir**, 2618m. From its southern shoreline climb steeply southwards in the direction of a small high ledge, then eastwards following the cairns across moraine, boulder fields and areas of old snow onto the **Col du Lac Noir**, 2869m. Descend on the other side into a hollow and at the foot of the border ridge, cross southwestwards towards a ridge of rock coming down from Pointe du Rocher Blanc. The tracks are quite feint that take you up onto this ridge with a bit of easy climbing (be careful, there

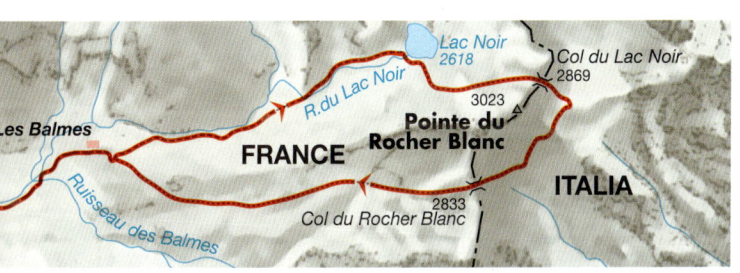

are some loose stones in places). A large cairn stands on the ridge, 2815m, to help with the route finding. Now cross some precipitous scree slopes in a southwesterly direction onto the Col du Rocher Blanc, 2833m. From the **Col du Rocher Blanc** descend into a small valley of moraine. Patches of snow remain here until well into high summer. Continue below the southern face of the Arête du Bêlier in a westerly direction, then across an open ridge with a magnificent view of the glacial tongues. Go past a ruin, towards the chalets of **Les Balmes** and back to **Chenal** down your ascent path.

23 Glacier de la Savinaz, 2300m

Glaciers and waterfalls high above the Haute-Tarentaise

La Gurraz – Refuge de la Martin – Glacier de la Savinaz and back

Starting point: La Gurraz, 1610m, car park at the entrance to the village and one as you leave (Parking du Chantal). Approach from Bourg-St-Maurice along the D 902 in the direction of Val d'Isère. Turn off right 2km after the cluster of houses of La Raie.

Walking times: La Gurraz – Refuge de la Martin 2 hrs., Refuge de la Martin – Glacier de la Savinaz a good ¼ hr., return just under 1¼ hrs.; total time 3½ hrs.

Height difference: about 700m.

Grade: easy mountain walk with a steep incline at the start.

Food and accommodation: Refuge de la Martin, staffed only July/Aug., always open, warden Marie-Claude Bonnevie, ✆ 04 79 06 44 32.

Alternative: you can walk from the Refuge de la Martin along a high trail with good views in 3 hrs. to Tignes. About half way along there's a turn-off to the Col de la Sachette: scenically beautiful crossing into the Vallon de Rosuel (3 hrs.; see Walk 18).

Map: IGN Top 25, sheet 3532 ET Les Arcs. La Plagne.

Waterfalls cascade down the huge steep rock faces behind the tiny picture-book village of La Gurraz. Rainbows flash through the spray. The broken start of a glacial tongue can be seen above with the summit of Mont Pourri lying hidden behind this. This is the remarkable sight at the start of the route which begins with a strenuous ascent. But once you have gained some height you can enjoy superb views high across the Haute-Tarentaise, with Mont Blanc drawing your attention in the north. Then it's only a hop, stride and a jump from the Refuge de la Martin to the enormous ice masses that flow down from the Dôme de la Sache.

From the furthest car park (Parking du Chantal) go first along a roadway to the left and southwards. Continue across the stream channel of the Ruisseau du Mont Pourri and zigzag steeply up onto an idyllic meadow to the ruins of **Grand Crêt**, 1906m. The best view is from the large cross on a small elevation on the left. The route now goes to the southwest into the furrow of the Ruisseau de la Savinaz. Cross the stream over a bridge construction secured with a cable below exciting cascades. Continue, only moderately ascending, across hillsides covered in broken rocks and onto the small plateau of the **Refuge de la Martin**, 2154m. A clear path sets off behind the hut on the right and ascends northwestwards round long bends through the moraine debris to the foot of the **Glacier de la Savinaz**, 2300m.

Return the same way.

The rugged tongue of the Glacier Sud de la Gurraz with Mont Pourri behind.

24 Lac de la Sassière, 2460m

Nature reserve rich in flora and fauna

Le Saut – Lac de la Sassière – Le Saut

The southern faces of Grande Sassière above the blossoming valley floor.

Starting point: Le Saut, 2280m, car park with info board. 5km from the eastern shore of Lac de Chevril, turn-off left after the 4th tunnel high above Villaret du Nial.
Walking times: Le Saut – Lac de la Sassière 1 hr., Lac de la Sassière – Le Saut ¾ hr.; total time 1¾ hrs.
Height difference: 180m.
Grade: comfortable family walk on good paths.
Food: none.
Alternatives: two pleasant walks go over passes from Lac de la Sassière to Val d'Isère: over the Passage de Picheru, 2760m, and the Col de la Bailletta, 2852m, both with a steep descent, but with wonderful views, 4½ hrs. For this you will also need the IGN Map 3633 ET Tignes. Val d'Isère.
Both passes can be linked together to make a challenging round walk, with the starting point in Val d'Isère. The approach from the reservoir to the Glacier de Rhêmes-Golette, 2½ hrs., is also impressive. All three routes go across alpine terrain where sure-footedness is essential.
Map: IGN Top 25, sheet 3532 ET Les Arcs. La Plagne.

The Sassière meanders through luxuriant shoreline meadows accompanied by abundantly flowering cotton grass. The southern faces of Grande Sassière tower up spectacularly above the left hand side of the valley. With a keen eye you might catch sight of the ibex and chamois. The many marmots to the left and right of the path are much less shy. As you look west you will see the reflection of the white sugar-coated summit of La Grande Motte in the small reservoir of Le Saut. The high valley, classified as the Réserve Naturelle de la Grande Sassière, is a feast for the eyes, the hiking path is broad and comfortable and from the Lac de la Sassière there are several high alpine hiking paths, enough to satisfy the tastes of every hiker.

La Grande Motte from Le Saut.

From the car park follow the leisurely roadway to the east upstream, past the **Chalet du Santel**, 2347m, and up a gentle incline to **Lac de la Sassière**, 2460m. Cross the dam and go right to the fork in the path. Go right again, now along the southern side of the valley over stony meadows, then close to the stream and finally around the small reservoir of **Le Saut**, back to the car park.

25 Col de la Rocheure, 2911m

Wild glacier country around the Pointes des Lorès

Le Manchet – Refuge du Fond des Fours – Col de la Rocheure – Les Pissets – Chalet du Riondet – Le Manchet

The Glacier des Fours.

Starting point: Le Manchet, 1957m, hamlet 5km south of Val d'Isère, car park just above.
Walking times: Le Manchet – Refuge du Fond des Fours 1¾ hrs., Refuge du Fond des Fours – Col de la Rocheure 2¼ hrs., Col de la Rocheure – Les Pissets ¾ hr., Les Pissets – Le Manchet 1¼ hrs.; total time 6 hrs.
Height difference: 954m.
Grade: you need a sense of direction from the Refuge because the path across the moraine is not always obvious (cairns), tricky when foggy; usually still a lot of patches of old snow in early summer.
Food and accommodation: Refuge du Fond des Fours, CAF, staffed middle of June to the middle of Sept., ✆ 04 79 06 16 90.
Map: IGN Top 25, sheet 3633 ET Tignes. Val d'Isère.

This walk goes through a wonderfully picturesque small high valley into barren moraine country at the foot of the glacier-covered Signal de Méan Martin. Close by the lunar landscape emerges as a magical rock garden, especially in July when it is covered with a reddish violet tinge, full of saxifrage, as well as arnica, sempervivum, gentian and silene. Then at the Col de la Rocheure you come to a broad high plateau brimming with shining lakes and surrounded by a sea of peaks.

From the car park go along the field path to the east until a path turns off right before the stream. Go upstream across stony meadows. Later go over a bridge and up a steep ledge onto a small plateau. After another steep ledge you come to the pretty Finnish houses of the **Refuge du Fond des Fours**, 2537m. Now carry on into the small high valley, the Vallon des Fours, but then turn off right at the fork in the path. Cross a stream and ascend steeply into the next high valley. Stay on the left hand bank, go across moraine towards the glacial slopes of Méan Martin in the south. Cairns guide you southwestwards across two streams. Climb steeply up onto a small col, 2917m, on the long north ridge coming down from Pointe de Méan Martin.

Continue uphill for a way to the west, then cross the slope of a band of rock, eventually over a wide, barren high plateau full of tiny lakes to the **Col de la Rocheure**, 2911m.

Continue along the GR 5 to the right down a scree slope into the increasingly verdant pastures. Go right at the fork of **Les Pissets**. Go across several streams, then descend sometimes steeply down the left hand side of the Vallon Pisset. An impressive waterfall thunders down half way along. The route continues from the **Chalet du Riondet** along a comfortable roadway northeastwards. Just before the gorge-like narrowing turn off the roadway, go over a small bridge. Go uphill again for a short way and on a left hand bend, go round the bouldering rock and back down to the car park.

26 Col de la Galise, 2987m

Window looking out to Gran Paradiso

Pont St-Charles – Gorges du Malpasset – Refuge de Prariond – Col de la Galise and back

Ibex in the Gorges du Malpasset.

Starting point: Pont St-Charles, 2056m, large car park with info board, 5km east of Val d'Isère on the road up to the Col de l'Iseran.
Walking times: Pont St-Charles – Refuge de Prariond 1¼ hrs., Refuge de Prariond – Col de la Galise 2 hrs., Col de la Galise – Pont St-Charles 1¾ hrs.; total time 5 hrs.
Height difference: 950m.
Grade: scree slopes on the ascent up to the pass; a glacier which is not dangerous and looks more like a large snowfield. You can usually cross the glacier without any problem, but towards the end of the season the covering of snow can be hard and slippery.
Food and accommodation: Refuge de Prariond, staffed 14.6.-14.9., ✆ 04 79 06 06 02
Alternative: at the fork at the Roche des Loses go right and ascend the Col de la Lose instead of the Col de la Galise, just as beautiful pass with views, and takes about the same amount of time.
Map: IGN Top 25, sheet 3633 ET Tignes. Val d'Isère.
Tip: crossing into Gran Paradiso National Park: descent to the Rifugio della Ballota (unstaffed, always open). For this you will need the IGN-Map Alpes sans Frontières, sheet 14 Vanoise, which covers the area over the border. Gran Paradiso.

You will already find the entrance into the high valley of Prariond sensational. The dramatically seething torrents of Isère have carved a deep trench

The Refuge de Prariond in the high valley of the same name.

into the Gorges du Malpasset. An old mule path balances through vertical gorge walls, used mostly in the late afternoon by Ibex sauntering along and not in a hurry to make way for the hiker. Quite unexpectedly the narrow pass opens out into a lovely green valley floor surrounded by rugged walls and the glaciers of the sources of the Isère shine out from the confusion of rocks in the east. The ascent then goes through a dolomitic-type mountain landscape onto the border ridge with Italy. The view into the Gran Paradiso massif and back down to Val d'Isère is truly breathtaking.

From the car park ascend steeply at first up the hillside to the east on the right hand side of the Isère, then on the level through the **Gorges du Malpasset** and onto the flat Prariond valley floor. After the furrow of a stream go to the **Refuge de Prariond**, 2324m, lying on the left just above. After the refuge climb up the steep grassy slope onto the mountain ridge of Grande Tête and eastwards to the fork at Roche des Loses, 2750m. Now cross a steep slope on the left, then go east again across moraine to the Glacier de la Galise. Go across the small snowfield, then up a schist slope onto the saddle of the **Col de la Galise**, 2987m. It's worth making the easy, but pathless summit ascent up to **Grand Cocor**, 3034m, at the south end of the border ridge from where the view is even more spectacular. Return the same way.

89

27 Refuge du Carro, 2759m

Panoramic path on the south balcony of the Col de l'Iseran

Pont de l'Oulietta – Plan des Eaux – Refuge du Carro and back

At your destination – the Refuge du Carro.

Starting point: Pont de l'Oulietta, 2476m, car park on the road up to the pass to the Col de l'Iseran.
Walking times: Pont de l'Oulietta – Plan des Eaux 1½ hrs., Plan des Eaux – Refuge du Carro 2¼ hrs., back 3¾ hrs.; total time 7½ hrs.
Height difference: 350m.
Grade: easy and more or less flat, but very long panoramic walk. A good walk for families if you make an overnight stop at the hut.
Food and accommodation: Refuge du Carro, CAF., staffed from the end of June to the end of Sept., ✆ 04 79 05 95 79.
Alternatives: two delightful, but steep ascents are possible from the hamlet of L'Ecot, via Le Saut, 2¾ hrs., and via La Tuilière, 2¼ hrs., as far as the Refuge du Carro.
Maps: IGN Top 25, sheet 3633 ET Tignes. Val d'Isère. Haute Maurienne; Didier Richard walking map 1:50,000, sheet 11 Vanoise.

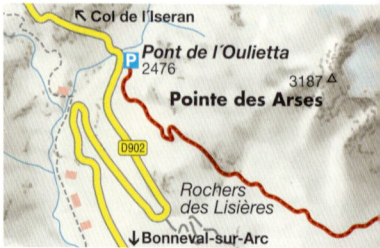

You can really enjoy the view of the border ridge of Haute Maurienne into Italy on this walk with a pleasant variation in height along the Sentier Balcon. The view of the Cirque des Evettes is impressive and l'Albaron and Grande Ciamarella tower up above. But the view close by is also very agreeable – luxuriant alpine pastures with curious marmots peeping out and the ringing of sheep bells, the ibex which even come quite close sometimes, small lively streams and cascading waterfalls. The highpoint is the two enchanting lakes nestling with their brilliant turquoise-blue into the cirque behind the Refuge du Carro.

From the car park follow the white and red Sentier Balcon to the south. You only gain a little height as you ascend round some bends, then the path descends to a boulder field and gently ascends again onto a meadow plateau running with small streams, marmots and sheep. The route loops round to the east to the lake of the **Plan des Eaux**, 2695m, and across the pastureland of Les Reys, 2664m. After a short steep incline up into a small high valley continue eastwards to the now visible **Refuge du Carro**, 2759m. It's a delightful walk around Lac Blanc (along some tracks) to the east of the hut.

Return the same way.

28 Cirque des Evettes, 2591m

A jumble of glaciers and an exciting gorge

L'Ecot – Refuge des Evettes – Gorge de la Reculaz – L'Ecot

Roman bridge between Bonneval and L'Ecot.

Starting point: Pont St-Clair, 2027m, car park at the hamlet of L'Ecot, about 4km from Bonneval-sur-Arc, 1850m, last village in the Haute Maurienne with bus service to Modane (station).
Walking times: L'Ecot – Refuge des Evettes 1¾ hrs., Refuge des Evettes – Gorge de la Reculaz – L'Ecot 1¾ hrs.; total time 3½ hrs.
Height difference: 564m.
Grade: not very long, but extremely demanding mountain walk requiring sure-footedness. A short section is made safe with cables and there is some easy climbing (I) in the upper part of the descent through the Gorge de la Reculaz, not advisable when wet.

Food and accommodation: Refuge des Evettes, July to the start of Sept., ✆ 04 79 05 96 64.
Alternative: pretty extension to the walk (1 hr. longer) by starting from Bonneval-sur-Arc: the mountain path on the northern bank of the Arc offers an idyllic gem along the way with the stone arch bridge of Pont de la Lama and crystal clear reservoirs where you can take an invigorating swim. You can continue this route to the source of the Arc (L'Ecot – Sources de l'Arc 3 hrs.).
Map: IGN Top 25, sheet 3633 ET Tignes. Val d'Isère. Haute Maurienne; Didier Richard walking map 1:50,000, sheet 11 Vanoise.

One of the best alpine mountain walks with spectacular diversity is offered along this relatively short route: glaciers, lakes, waterfalls. The highlight is the glacial amphitheatre of the rock basin, the Cirque des Evettes, as well as the Gorge de la Reculaz where there's some real climbing to be done in the upper section. Precipitous rock faces plummet into the deep gorge through which a huge waterfall thunders down.

From the hiker's park before **Pont St-Clair**, 2027m, a well-trodden mountain path winds its way up the northern hillside. Keep left at all the following turn-offs. Wide and narrow zigzag paths lead up the steep incline over open meadows and broken terrain into the high Evettes valley. The last section gradually levels out and ends on a grassy knoll. The spectacle which awaits you here is breathtaking – reminiscent of the Himalaya! Countless tiny deep blue and turquoise lakes lie shimmering in an enormous rock basin, a river meanders through the wide scree basin, bursting glacial streams flow down craggy mountain sides. The Glacier des Evettes is surrounded by Pic Regaud, 3232m, and Albaron, 3637m, in the west, by Petite, 3537m, and Grande Ciamarella, 3676m, in the south, by Pointe Tonini, 3327m, Pointe de Séa, 3213m, and Pointe de Bonneval, 3320m, in the east. Immediately on the left from where you are standing you can see the nearby **Refuge des Evettes**, 2590m, high above four small lakes. The cosy accommodation is decorated inside with lots of colourful prayer flags. If wind and weather are permitting, you can sit outside on the splendid terrace.

Five minutes below the hut a signpost indicates the way to the **Cascade de la Reculaz**. It's worth making the ten minute detour to the seething waterfall. Otherwise keep to the left. It's now a steep and abrupt descent over scree

and grassy ledges. The most difficult passages of the steep ledge are secured with cables and lead to the sometimes overhanging edge of the gorge. There's a dizzying view of the thundering masses of water below. The ice field of the Glacier du Grand Méan you can see glistening in the east. The route now follows the steep bank without any great difficulties and then descends scree to the flat bank area. The path along the bank is lined with bushes at first and after joining the Arc valley runs across marvellous meadows back to the **car park**.

93

29 Refuge d'Avérole, 2229m

Fabulous walk through a picture-book valley

Vincendières – Avérole – Refuge d'Avérole – Vincendières

Starting point: car park at Vincendières, 1830m. Turn off the D 902 at Pont Neuf between Bessans and Villaron, 3km.
Walking times: Vincendières – Avérole 1 hr., Avérole – Refuge d'Avérole 1 hr., Refuge d'Avérole – Vincendières 1 hr., total time 3 hrs.
Height difference: 400m.
Grade: easy walk, suitable for families, on comfortable paths, only the last section to the refuge is steep.
Food and accommodation: Refuge d'Avérole, CAF, staffed end of June to the beginning of Sept., ✆ 04 79 05 96 70.
Alternatives: a delightful alpine circular walk starts at the Refuge d'Avérole and goes along the right hand bank of the Torrent de Lombarde up to the Pas de la Mule, 2350m. Return along the left hand bank to the car park at Vincendières; 4½ hrs. Start in Bessans along the Sentier nature to the edge of the forest, then on the left hand bank of the Torrent d'Avérole to Avérole, 3 hrs.
Maps: IGN Top 25, sheet 3633 ET Tignes. Val d'Isère. Or IGN Alpes sans Frontières, sheet 13, Mont-Cenis. Ciamarella.

The Avérole valley is an idyllic place with its unspoilt scenery and where you come across ancient hamlets in the typical architectural style for the Haute-Maurienne. Chapels and wayside crosses line the paths. The location of the Refuge d'Avérole is unique. From here you can gaze across the Bessanese, 3592m, and the surrounding landscape of glaciers with little streams and waterfalls.

Looking back towards Avérole and the valley of the same name.

Contented cows near Avérole.

From **Vincendières**, 1830m, continue along the roadway, then on the hiking path which runs parallel to it past the Oratoire St-Antoine du Bec and leads up a moderate incline to **Avérole**, 1990m. Pass through the hamlet and past the Oratoire Notre Dame de la Garde along the right hand side of the valley up to the **Refuge d'Avérole**, 2229m, visible from afar. Return the same way to point 2077 where a path branches off to a bridge. Go along the other side of the stream to the right, now on the left hand side of the Torrent d'Avérole, as far as the bridge at **Vincendières** and back to the car park.

30 Rochemelon, 3538m

A 'pilgrim's' trek onto the highest pilgrimage mountain in Europe

Bessans – Vallée du Ribon – Glacier de Rochemelon – Rochemelon and back

Starting point: Bessans, 1705m, holiday resort in the Haute-Maurienne, or the small car park at the start of the Ribon valley.
Walking times: Bessans – Vallée du Ribon 1½ hrs., Vallée du Ribon – Glacier de Rochemelon 3 hrs., Glacier de Rochemelon – Rochemelon 2 hrs., Rochemelon – Bessans 4½ hrs.; total time 11 hr.
Height difference: 1833m.
Grade: high alpine walk that demands some experience of glaciers although the Glacier de Rochemelon is relatively easy to cross due to it being flat and having only a few crevasses. Sometimes crampons are needed, so be sure to take them with you! If you approach Rochemelon from Bessans and plan to return the same day, you will need to be super fit.
Food: none.
Accommodation: hotels in Bessans.
Map: IGN-Map 1:25,000, sheet 3634 OT Mont Cenis or IGN Alpes sans Frontières, sheet 13.
Tips: the pilgrimage takes place every year on 5. August, as well as on Assumption Day on 15. Aug. Information obtainable from the tourist office.
The approach from Susa on the Italian side is easier.

The way down from the summit of Rochemelon.

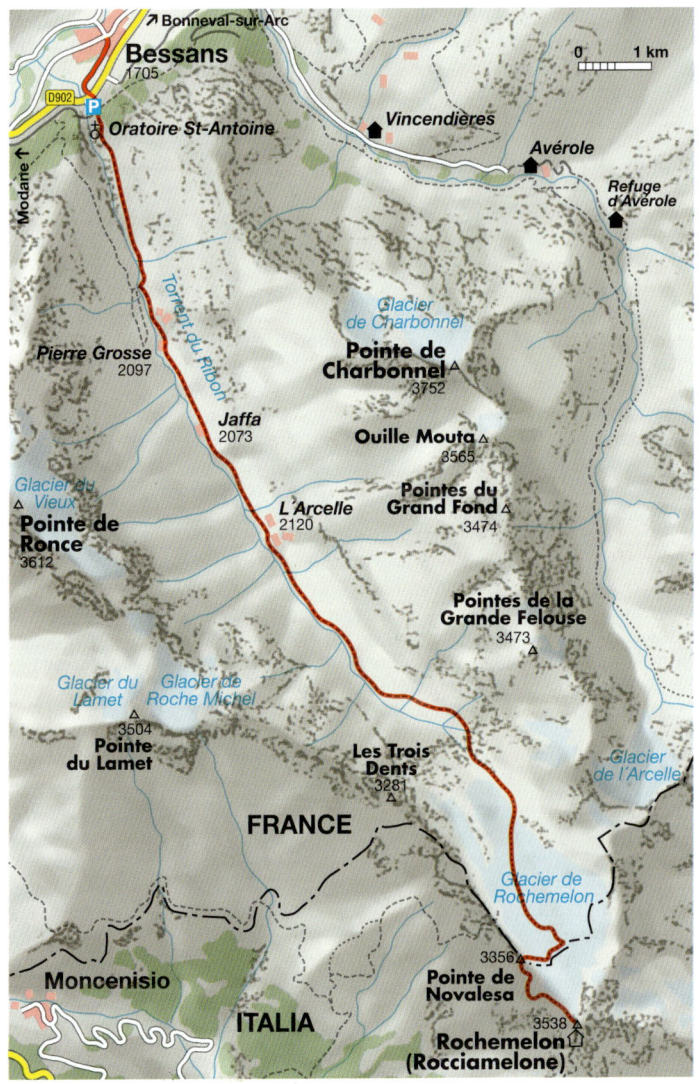

The 5. August gives rise to an unusual mountain walk every year. It is the day of the Madonna of the snow and people pay their homage on top of the 3538m high Rochemelon. The locals make a pilgrimage from the French and Italian high valleys to the huge bronze Madonna situated on the highest mountain in the Piedmont.

From the heart of the village of **Bessans** (1705m) go along the D 902 ring road and (in a westerly direction) soon turn left onto the first little road that zigzags southwards steeply up the first high shelf into the **Vallée du Ribon**. On the way up your attention is drawn to the prayer chapels of St-Antoine and St-Anne, the two saints being the patron saints of the valley. The broad gravel path then ascends a gentle, almost leisurely incline and soon becomes into a hiking path. This path continues on the right hand bank of the Ribon a long way up to the head of the valley. On the way you pass the alpine mountain huts of **Les Chalets de Pierre Grosse** (2097m), then the huts of Jaffa and Saulcier, later those of l'Arcelle (2120m). After point 2322 the mountain path ascends steeply again, goes south-eastwards up a moraine ridge to the foot of a steep ledge. Cross the Ribon stream over to the right and afterwards there's some easy climbing over rocky ledges and gravel towards the glacier. Now descend easily to the glacier. The views are becoming more and more breathtaking. It's a fantastic spectacle in the north with the sea of peaks in the Vanoise National Park. La Grande Casse, La Grande Motte and Mont Pourri are the highest protagonists in this rock drama. Cross the Glacier de Rochemelon right down the middle with your destination of the summit of the Rochemelon always in sight in the south. Just before reaching its north flank go right and up along a steep gravel path onto the north ridge. Continue along this ridge to eventually reach the summit of **Rochemelon** (3538m), crowned by the three metre high figure of the Madonna.

The view is awesome. Which ever way you turn there's a range of mountains reaching right up to the horizon. A chapel is to be found in the summit hut. Amongst the countless votive pictures you will also find the copy of the legendary triptych that is supposed to have been erected here in 1358 by a certain Bonifacio Rotario d'Asti. It is said that the alleged crusader fell into the hands of the Muslims and made a pledge to build a holy site on the highest peak in the Piedmont in the event of his liberation. The existence of this man was indeed documented, but he was not a crusader because the crusades had taken place a long time before that. However, this nebulous story endorses the myth and makes this mountain that is shrouded in mystery even more appealing.

Return the same way.

Glacier de Rochemelon with Mont Pourri in the background.

31 Pierre aux Pieds, 2750m

To the most famous boulder with imprints in the Maurienne

Le Collet – Refuge de Vallonbrun – Pierre aux Pieds and back

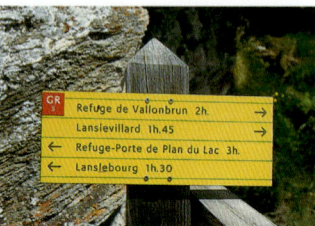

Starting point: Le Collet, 1752m, hamlet on the Col de la Madeleine between Bessans and Lanslevillard. Car park at the chapel.
Walking times: Le Collet – Refuge de Vallonbrun 1¾ hrs., Refuge de Vallonbrun – Pierre aux Pieds 2 hrs., descent to Le Collet 1¾ hrs.; total time 5½ hrs.
Height difference: 1020m.
Grade: hiking path with steep ascent and descent.
Accommodation: Refuge de Vallonbrun, 14.6.-14.9., ✆ 04 79 05 93 93, hut warden Michelle Arnaud, ✆ 79 05 88 21.
Map: IGN Top 25, sheet 3633 ET, Tignes.

Val d'Isère.
Tip: you can extend the walk from the Plan de la Cha (at the turn-off to the Pierre aux Pieds) along the GR 5. The high trail has beautiful views and runs up a moderate incline via the Refuge du Cuchet (1¼ hrs., hut always open, unstaffed; steep descent to Lanslebourg 1½ hrs.), continue to the Refuge du Plan du Lac (4 hrs.; ✆ 04 79 20 37 12), then via the Refuge de l'Arpont (8 hrs.; ✆ 04 79 20 51 51), etc.
It's recommended that you start this long distance walk along the GR 5 in Bessans (Bessans – Le Collet 1 hr.) so that you can return by bus.

Pierre aux Pieds has been declared an historic monument since 1911. People are still puzzling over the origin of the imprints in this huge boulder which stands in an isolated position below the craggy summit of Grand Roc Noir. Scientists date the rock to the time of the iron age between 700 and

The mysterious Pierre aux Pieds with its holes and footprints.

200 BC. 82 small footprints between 80 holes form a pattern on the surface of the erratic block. All of them point to the east from where the sun throws its first golden light on the striking chain of mountains. Did religious rites take place here perhaps? A sun cult? Was homage paid to the gods of the mountains? They still haven't revealed their secret…

From the **chapel of Marie-Madeleine**, 1752m, ascend the southern slope up the steep zigzags of the GR 5 until you reach a high terrace with beautiful views and the Chapelle St-Antoine, 2321m. The pretty **Refuge de Vallonbrun**, 2272m, lies to the west just below. Go right at the fork there in a westerly direction across the hillside until the path forks again. Continue right in a semi-circle around the channel of the Ruisseau du Diet to the sloping meadows of **Les Marmottières**, 2500m. Zigzag up a steep shelf and go a short way across the southeastern face of Grand Roc Noir to the **Pierre aux Pieds**, 2750m.

Return the same way.

32 Pointe de Lanserlia, 2909m

Summit in the heart of the Vanoise with wonderful views

Bellecombe car park – Col de Lanserlia – Pointe de Lanserlia – Refuge du Plan du Lac – Bellecombe

Starting point: Bellecombe car park, 2387m, furthest point (for private vehicles) on the D 126, 14km from Termignon, turn-off from the N 6 on the sharp right hand bend.
Walking times: Bellecombe car park – Col de Lanserlia 1½ hrs., Col de Lanserlia – Pointe de Lanserlia ½ hr., Pointe de Lanserlia – Refuge du Plan du Lac 2 hrs., Refuge du Plan du Lac – Bellecombe ½ hr.; total time 4½ hrs.
Height difference: 550m.
Grade: easy mountain walk which requires you to have a sense of direction. Patches of old snow in June.
Accommodation: Refuge du Plan du Lac, staffed from the end of May to the end of Sept., ✆ 04 79 20 50 85.
Map: IGN Top 25, sheet 3633 ET, Tignes. Val d'Isère. Haute Maurienne.

The gleaming glacial tongues and mountains all around the luxuriantly green plateau of Plan du Lac are as radiant as the smile of Anne-Marie Pelissier, the 'oldest' hut warden in France, who is turning her back unfortunately on the Refuge du Plan du Lac after 31 years to run a B&B in the Ténéré desert. What remains is the nice and cosy hut with a fantastic view. The nearby mountain is Pointe de Lanserlia with its long, striking ridge directly behind the hut to the east. A magnificent view opens up from the top there: the volcanic-like world of Grand Roc Noir in the north, Dent Parrachée, Dôme de l'Arpont, Dôme de Chasseforêt in the west, the glacial tongues of the Vanoise glaciers in between, the huge south face of

Plan du Lac from Pointe de Lanserlia.

Grande Casse in the north. In the foreground the dark rock wall of Pointes de Pierre Brune separates the barren valleys of the Leisse and the Rocheure. The fascinating and bizarre rock towers of Rochers de Lanserlia lie directly at your feet.

From **Bellecombe** car park, 1387m, take the broad field path to the right and follow the white and red marked GR 5 to just beyond the Chalet Alpage de Piou. Go left at the cairn onto the path that ascends at first to the east, but then turns off to the north and runs up across meadows to the **Col de Lanserlia**, 2774m. The views into Val d'Arc to the south are spectacular and of the mountain range of Mont Cenis, and Dent Parrachée is really close by in the west. Go slightly to the left from the pass to the first lake. From there ascend westwards to the ridge and continue along here to the right to **Pointe de Lanserlia**, 2909m.

From the summit follow tracks onto the small col, 2842m, before **Rochers de Lanserlia** (where it's worth making a detour to the summit, 10 minutes). Descend right across undulating hills into the Grand Vallon where you meet the hiking path again close to the stream. Follow this path towards the Vallon de la Rocheure until a path branches off left that takes you on the level and with beautiful views to the **Refuge du Plan du Lac**, 2384m. Continue left along the GR 5 back to the car park.

33 Plan du Lac – Sentier Balcon de l'Arpont

Circular panoramic walk below huge glaciers

Pont du Chatelard – Le Coêtet – Lac Blanc – Refuge du Lac Blanc – Refuge du Plan du Lac – Renaudière – Lacs des Lozières – Refuge de l'Arpont – Le Mont – Pont du Chatelard

Refuge du Lac Blanc.

Starting point: Pont du Châtelard car park, 1347m, on the D 83, 2km from Termignon.
Also possible: Bellecombe car park, 2387m, end of the road (for private traffic) on the D 126, 14km from Termignon, turn-off from the N 6 on the sharp right hand bend.
There's a daily shuttle bus from the 28.6. to 31.8. ('navette') from Termignon or the Bellecombe car park to Entre Deux Eaux (see map). Bellecombe car park – Entre Deux Eaux 7.45 to 17.45 (saves you 1 hr. of walking), Termignon – Bellecombe car park – Entre Deux Eaux only 7.15, 9.00, 13.30.
Walking times: Pont du Châtelard – Le Coêtet 2 hrs., Le Coêtet – Refuge du Lac Blanc 1 hr., Refuge du Lac Blanc – car park Bellecombe ¼ hr., car park Bellecombe – Refuge du Plan du Lac ½ hr., Refuge du Plan du Lac – Lacs des Lozières 2½ hrs., Lacs des Lozières – Refuge de l'Arpont 2 hrs., Refuge de l'Arpont – Pont du Chatelard 1½ hrs.; total time 9¾ hrs.
Height difference: 1600m.
Grade: 2 day walk or long mountain walk with the use of shuttle buses. Some steep sections demand sure-footedness and a good level of fitness.
Food and accommodation: Refuge du Lac Blanc, 2300m, staffed middle of June to the end of Sept., ✆ 06 84 04 23 36; Refuge du Plan du Lac, 2384m, staffed end of March to end of Sept., ✆ 04 79 20 50 85; Refuge de l'Arpont, 2309m, staffed middle of June to middle of Sept., ✆ 04 79 20 51 51.
Alternatives: 1) If, instead of ascending via Lac Blanc/Refuge du Lac Blanc, you prefer to approach the Refuge du Plan du Lac directly (1 hr. shorter), stay on the path from the shrine of the Virgin Mary at the Oratoire St-Antoine, 2023m, that keeps parallel to the D 126.
2) From the Refuge de l'Arpont you can extend the walk as far as Aussois along the GR 5 with fantastic views in 5½ hrs. (see Walks 34, 35, 36, 37, 38). Or in the opposite direction from Bellecombe car park along the GR 5 in 5½ hrs. to the Refuge de Vallonbrun (see Walk 27) and to Bessans (see Walks 28, 29).
Map: IGN Top 25, sheet 3633 ET, Tignes. Val d'Isère. Haute Maurienne.

Termignon offers one of the most impressive gateways into the Vanoise National Park. Around the deep gorge of the river of the same name there are some marvellous high plateaus and viewing terraces to be explored along a striking panoramic path. Along the way you will find pretty accommodation and crystal clear mountain lakes in which the Vanoise glacier and its huge peaks are reflected. Lovely undulating meadows, but also rugged moraine country and exhausting ups-and-downs make this walk into a very varied and adventurous experience.

View of Grande Casse from the Refuge du Plan du Lac.

Plan du Lac with Grande Casse.

From the car park at the **Pont du Chatelard**, 1347m, follow the D 83 about another 600m to the Pont du Villard, 1398m. A hiking path beyond the bridge leads steeply up along the right hand side of the Baches Chavière through a light forest. After a rock shelf with bizarre rock towers a link path goes to the left in the direction of Lac Blanc to the hiking path which starts from the nearby car park at Le Coëtet. From the **Refuge du Lac Blanc**, 2300m, follow the field path northeastwards to **Bellecombe car park**, 2387m, and onto the white and red marked GR 5 parallel to the road. Go past the Refuge du Plan du Lac, 2384m, and the Chapelle St-Barthélémy, 2284m, down to **Pont de la Renaudière**, 2053m. Descend west to the small weir, go over a bridge to the chalets of l'Ile and up a zigzag path across grassy slopes to the fork at **Mont de la Para**, 2329m. Continue left and quickly gain height. The Sentier Balcon now goes leisurely round a semi-circle at first through the moraine landscape of the Glacier du Pelve with the idyllic **Lacs des Lozières**, 2479m, then along a high ledge above the deeply indented gorge of Doron de Termignon to the **Refuge de l'Arpont**, 2309m. A worthwhile detour takes 1 hr. to Lac de l'Arpont. From the Refuge de l'Arpont continue along the white and red GR 5 to the south, then at the Le Mont chalet turn off left. Steeply descend the wide bends via the alpine mountain huts of **Esseillon**, 1780m, to the **Pont du Châtelard**, 1347m.

34 Le Sentier des Bâtisseurs

On the trail of soldiers and impressive forts

Fort Marie-Christine – Fort Charles-Albert – Pont du Diable – Fort Victor-Emmanuel – Fort Marie-Christine

Starting point: Fort Marie-Christine, 1486m (also possible from Fort Charles-Albert or Fort Victor-Emmanuel), 1km below Aussois, 1500m, bus service with Modane (station).
Walking times: Fort Marie-Christine – Fort Charles-Albert – Ancien Pont du Diable 1½ hrs., Ancien Pont du Diable – Fort Victor-Emmanuel – Fort Marie-Christine 1½ hrs.; total time 3 hrs.
Height difference: 400m.

Grade: leisurely circular walk along a nature trail.
Food: none.
Accommodation: Hotel du Soleil (Relais du Silence), directly by the church of Aussois, with sauna and wonderful roof terrace with whirlpool, ✆ 04 79 20 32 42; Gîte d'Étape in the Fort Marie-Christine, ✆ 04 79 20 36 44.
Map: IGN Top 25, sheet 3534 OT, Les Trois Vallée. Modane.
Tips: at the Parc Archéologie des Lozes (about 1km east of Aussois) there's an exhibition of prehistoric rock imprints (gravures rupestres). You can take a pleasant half hour round walk through the meadows with beautiful views.
Other nature trails that branch off from the Sentier des Bâtisseurs are the Sentier du Plateau d'Aussois, a link between the Fort Marie-Christine and the Fort Charles-Albert, waymarked in green, ½ hr., Sur les traces du Marabout, starting point is the Sardinian cemetery, waymarked in green, 1½ hrs. and Sous le Soleil d'Avrieux, a short walk around Avrieux, which incorporates the scenically delightful waterfall, the Cascade St-Benoît, waymarked in blue, 1 hr.

Under the name of 'Les Sentiers de l'Esseillon' several nature trails wind their way through the vast area of forts of Esseillon that was set up between 1817 and 1834 by the Sardinian crown for the purpose of defending a feared invasion over the Mont-Cenis-Pass. The most interesting and longest nature trail 'Le Sentier des Bâtisseurs' (7½km) goes on the trail of the soldiers through picturesque scenery and links all five Forts de l'Esseillon. They are built onto terraces in the slopes and balance spectacularly above the dramatic Arc gorge and immediately attract your attention on the drive there. Fort Marie-Christine is both the starting and finishing point. It is the highest fort of them all and, together with accommodation, also houses an information centre for the Vanoise National Park.

From Fort **Marie-Christine** (1486m) go along a hiking path parallel to the road to Fort Charles-Albert (1508m) situated in the east. The Sentier des Bâtisseurs continues to go south through prairie grass to a quarry, then westwards to the Sardinian cemetery, the **Cimetière Sarde**. Continue onto the forest path on the other side of the road which zigzags uphill through a marvellous pine forest to an excellent stopping point with views. Now descend through the forest and meadows with good views and full of cypress trees to a fork where you keep left and soon reach the **Hameau de l'Esseillon** (1300m), the former barracks of the non-commissioned officers. Go down across the meadow on the left of a stone obelisk onto a broad field path which you follow right. Very soon after that signposts indicate to the left. The forest path descends leisurely and then goes round a sharp right hand bend to the right. Here you will find a viewpoint of the Arc gorge and the quarry of **Carrière de Lauze**. Stone was quarried here for building the forts. The forest path now runs above the Arc gorge until signs point you towards the next highlight – the remains of the old bridge, **Ancien Pont du Diable** (1195m).

The path ascends again gently and winds round a groove which offers views of the new Pont du Diable. After descending a few metres you come to a marvellous picnic spot. At the fork beyond it's a pleasant five minute detour left to the **Pont du Diable** (1155m) with the famous view far below down into the gorge where you can watch the climbers on the via ferrata (see Walk 35). On the other side of the bridge the Redoute Marie-Thérèse is soon reached which houses a museum. The well-trodden zigzag path goes to the right in 20 minutes up to the Fort **Victor-Emmanuel** (1354m).

From the car park (1215m) go to the left (north) up a short steep incline and follow the path along the crest of the ridge. Go round below the ruins of Fort **Charles-Félix** and continue northwards along the ridge to Fort **Marie-Christine**.

One of the most pleasant via ferrata begins at the Fort Victor-Emmanuel.

35 Via ferrata du Diable

A thrilling route through the gorge with exciting views far below

Fort Victor-Emmanuel – Passerelle des Enfers – Montée au Purgatoire – Traversée des Anges – Pont du Diable – Montée au Ciel – Fort Victor-Emmanuel

Starting point: Fort Victor-Emmanuel, 1354m, the impressive fort complex high above the Arc gorge, 3km below Aussois, 1500m, bus service with Modane (station).
Other possible starting points are Redoute Marie-Thérèse on the N6, 7km from Modane, or between Villarobin and Arvieux via the Via ferrata du Chemin de la Vierge (access also via the forest path on the RN 6 1km before the Redoute), info board in each place.
Walking times: Fort Victor-Emmanuel – Descente aux Enfers 1 hr., Descente aux Enfers – Montée au Purgatoire 1 hr., Montée au Purgatoire – Traversée des Anges 1 hr., Traversée des Anges – Fort Victor-Emmanuel 1 hr.; total time 4 hrs., if it's busy, the route can take 6 hrs.
Height difference: Descente aux Enfers: 170m descent, Montée au Purgatoire: 110m ascent, Traversée des Anges: 40m descent, Montée au Ciel: 120m ascent; in total: 230m ascent, 210m descent.

Grade: demanding and especially long sport via ferrata which can be done in several distinct sections (from fairly to very difficult). Some very airy traverses, a few short, but cracking overhangs, two suspension bridges.
Accommodation: Hotel du Soleil (Relais du Silence), directly next to the church of Aussois, with sauna and marvellous roof terrace with whirlpool, ✆ 04 79 20 32 42; Fort Marie-Christine, ✆ 04 79 20 36 44.
Map: IGN Top 25, sheet 3534 OT Les Trois Vallée. Modane.
Tip: hiring of via ferrata equipment: Sport 2000 in Aussois, ✆ 04 79 20 31 11. A varied via ferrata has been specially created around the fort for children and beginners. Without any noticeable height variation it consists of two parts – Les Angelots, 400m in length, about 1 hr. and Les Diablotins, 500m long, 1-2 hrs.
On certain days in July and August the Fort Victor-Emmanuel is alight with a 'son et lumière spectacle' from 21.30.

Undoubtedly the most unusual via ferrata in the Maurienne, extremely exposed, but excellently secured and without the most severe level of difficulties. It comprises seven routes which can be done independently from one another. With a total length of 3460m it is the longest via ferrata in the whole of France and is a gem for via ferrata enthusiasts who, at the same time, are able to admire one of the most delightful gorges. Its special gimmick is that the start and end of the via ferrata is a fort dating from the 18th century, which can also be climbed round on a children's route.

From the car park enter the **Fort Victor-Emmanuel** (1354m) and go down some steps to the lowest level of the huge fort complex. An info board marks the window through which you have to crawl to reach the start of the **Descente aux Enfers**. Follow the cables to the right. At first go along a narrow shelf of rock along the fort wall, then down a steep dirt path (slippery!) into the forest and to a sheer drop which opens up a fabulous view into the Arc gorge. Descend diagonally at first on iron rungs then vertically and finally over a slight overhang to the **Passerelle des Enfers**. The **Montée au Purgatoire** begins after the wonderful suspension bridge. Ascend stepped rock diagonally upwards to the Cascade du Nant. Go through the spray of the waterfall on a vertical line which ends in a slight overhang. The Chemin de la Vierge via ferrata joins from the right over a suspension bridge. From here you can also descend to Avrieux (1½ hrs.). Otherwise keep left and along a good mountain path reach the Redoute Marie-Thérèse (1260m).

On the Via ferrata du Diable.

The continuation of the route, the so-called **Traversée des Anges**, is signposted at the viewing rock just before reaching the fort museum. Descend a few metres diagonally, then begin an extremely exposed traverse which demands not only strength in your arms, but also nerves of steel. There is, however, an escape route half way along. You finally reach the wooded plateau again via a short vertical drop. Go left along the broad forest path and soon afterwards come to the famous devil's bridge from where there's usually a crowd of spectators looking down in amazement on the climbers on the via ferrata. After the **Pont du Diable** (1155m) a gate on the right marks the approach to the **Montée au Ciel**. Safety ropes lead you under the bridge, then diagonally to vertically, sometimes slightly overhanging, up to the **Fort Victor-Emmanuel** where you slip through the window again.

36 La Turra – Trou de la Lune, 2650m

Bizarre limestone formations and a large rock gateway

Aussois – Monolithe de Sardières – La Turra – Trou de la Lune – La Turra – Plateau des Arponts – Gorges St-Pierre – Aussois

Starting point: Aussois, 1480m, or Plan de la Croix car park, 1km von Aussois, or the car park at the Monolithe de Sardières, 1895m, 4km from Aussois, both in the direction of Sardières.

Walking times: Aussois – Monolithe de Sardières 1 hr., Monolithe de Sardières – La Turra 3 hrs., La Turra – Trou de la Lune 1 hr., Trou de la Lune – Plateau des Arponts 2 hrs., Plateau des Arponts – Gorges St-Pierre ½ hr., Gorges St-Pierre – Aussois ½ hr.; total time 8 hrs.

Height difference: 1170m.

Grade: a short passage on the ascent between the forest boundary and the GR 5 is rather exposed and slippery. The detour from La Turra to the rock gateway Trou de la Lune is unmarked and at times without paths and the last part to the foot of the face is tricky, especially slippery on the descent.

Food: none.

Accommodation: Hotel du Soleil (Relais du Silence), directly next to the church of Aussois, with sauna and wonderful roof terrace with whirlpool, ✆ 04 79 20 32 42.

Alternative: you can extend the walk along the beautiful high trail of the GR 5 from La Turra in 4½ hrs. as far as the Refuge de l'Arpont (see Walk 33).

Map: IGN Top 25, sheet 3534 OT, Les Trois Vallées. Modane.

The Monolithe de Sardières, a 93 metre high rock needle that towers up conspicuously from the coniferous forest, is one of the special attractions of Aussois. If you're lucky you will be able to watch climbers testing themselves on the three bolted routes. If you ascend through the forest you will be enchanted by the picturesque landscape where erosion has created some bizarre rock formations. The magnificent and striking pinnacle of Roc des Corneilles, in which there's a rock gateway, affords you breathtaking views a long way below. The elongated valley of the Haute-Maurienne lies at your feet and the white jagged pinnacles of the Ecrins jut out above the sea of peaks in the southwest. The highpoint of the return is the narrow, idyllic Gorges St-Pierre.

From **Aussois**, 1480m, follow the main road in the direction of Sardières. At the cross and car park of Plan de la Croix continue along the side road as far as the bouldering area on a sharp right hand bend. The Sentier du Milieu turns off here to the left. The path runs parallel to the road through dense forest to the **Monolithe de Sardières**, 1695m. From the car park follow the field path uphill to the west. At the next

Trou de la Lune.

fork go right to the Source de Fournette. Continue up along a drivable track just above. Unmarked steep side paths take shortcuts across the loops. At the forest boundary take the path to the left that at first crosses under some rocks and then meets the GR 5 below Grasse Combe. Go for a short way right along this path up the steep gully, then go to the right around a corner rock and onto the small plateau of **La Turra**, 2363m.

Continue to follow the GR 5 for a way. At the third large bend, about 2450m, ascend left onto the ridge of the meadow which runs down in a southeasterly direction from the striking rock of Roc des Corneilles. Later on you will see some tracks in the dusty scree which climb up steeply and exposed to the east facing rock wall. At the foot of the wall you find yourself standing unexpectedly in front of the gaping hole in the rock of **Trou de la Lune**, 2650m, which forms a photogenic frame for the Rateau d'Aussois close by in the west.

Return the same way to the meadow hollow of **La Turra**. Then go eastwards around the rock face of La Turra and return through a light coniferous forest to the crossroads at the forest boundary. Reverse your ascent path, but do not turn off left to the source, continue to follow the forest path instead. Go left at the second turn-off along a track, not at the signpost for Arponts. Go along the edge of the **Plateau des Arponts**, past two chalets, then turn right onto the narrow path before a left hand bend. This path crosses the wooded slope via **Gorges St-Pierre** and then descends to the stream below. After crossing the stream a wooden sign indicates left along the path into the gorge which runs over several tiny bridges and wooden planks through the increasingly narrow canyon. You re-emerge at the bridge of **Le Coin**, 1490m, just outside **Aussois**.

37 Pointe de l'Observatoire, 3015m

Viewing summit on the border ridge of the Tarentaise and the Maurienne

Plan d'Amont – Refuge du Fond d'Aussois – Col d'Aussois – Pointe de l'Observatoire – Refuge de la Dent Parrachée – Refuge la Fournache – Plan d'Amont

The Refuge de la Dent Parrachée.

Starting point: Plan d'Amont, 2050m, car park at the dam. Approach from Aussois along the D 108E.
The start is also possible from Aussois by chairlift (Télésiège du Grand Jeu, Aussois-Montana, 30.6. – 29.8., Mon – Fr 9.00 – 11.45, 14.00 – 17.45). Bus service to Modane (station).
Walking times: Plan d'Amont – Refuge du Fond d'Aussois 1 hr., Refuge du Fond d'Aussois – Col d'Aussois 2 hrs., Col d'Aussois – Pointe de l'Observatoire ½ hr., Pointe de l'Observatoire – Refuge du Fond d'Aussois 1½ hrs., Refuge du Fond d'Aussois – Refuge de la Dent Parrachée ¾ hr., Refuge de la Dent Parrachée – Plan d'Amont 1 hr.; total time 6¾ hrs.
Height difference: 1160m, if the descent is the same as the ascent: 970m.
Grade: some easy climbing on the last few metres to the summit (I).
Food and accommodation: Refuge du Fond d'Aussois, ✆ 04 79 20 39 83, Refuge de la Dent Parrachée, ✆ 04 79 20 32 87; Refuge la Fournache, ✆ 06 09 38 72 38, each of them staffed 15.6. – 15.9.
Alternative: in midsummer there could be a lot of traffic on the paths between the refuges. You can walk one level higher along a usually more isolated path (because it is not marked on the IGN Maps) and with a brilliant view. For this you ascend from the Pont de la Sétéria to the left in the direction of Col de la Masse to a high shelf with a fork in the path. A path branches off right just below marked with cairns, crosses the hillside strewn with boulders to the Refuge du Fond d'Aussois.
Map: IGN Top 25, sheet 3534 OT, Les Trois Vallées. Modane.

Aussois church.

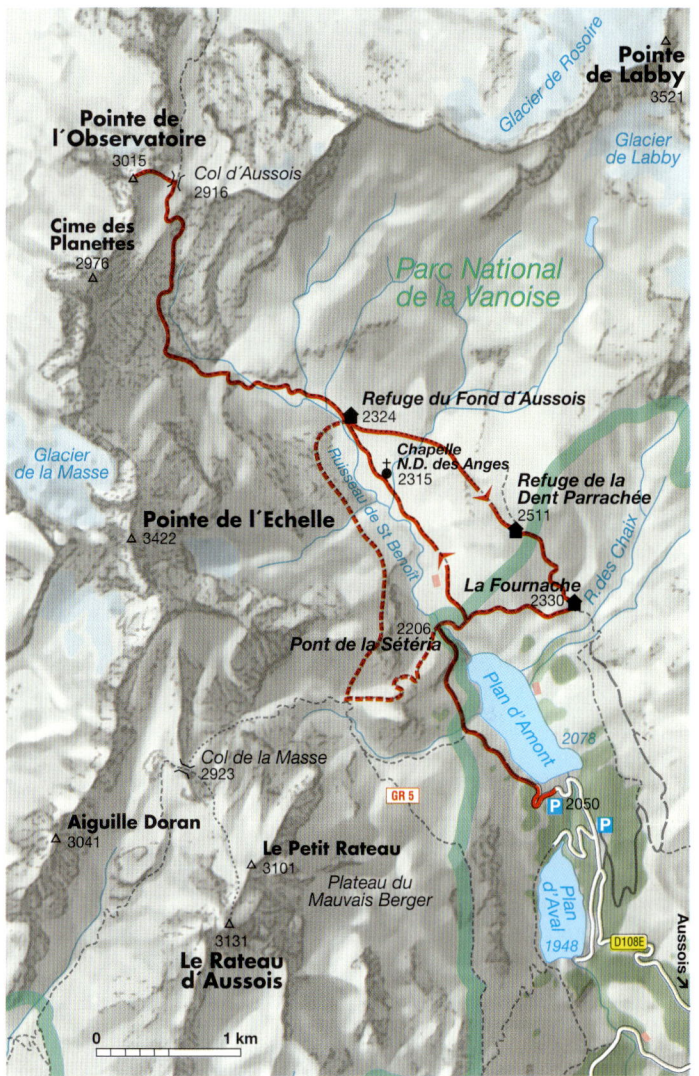

On the way up from the Fond d'Aussois to the Col d'Aussois.

In the Vanoise massif there are many easily climbed 3000ers, but none of them reveal such a magnificent view as Pointe de l'Observatoire. The impressive views down into the Tarentaise take your breath away especially. The north and west faces plummet down vertically into the bottomless abyss. The turquoise blue Lac Blanc shines up from below and Dôme de Polset towers above it with the Glacier de Gébroulaz. The extensive array of peaks in the north is dominated by Mont Blanc. The Vanoise glaciers, bordered by Pointe de Labby and Dent Parrachée, glisten in the east. In the south can be seen the huge mountains at the border with Italy.

Go along the broad hiking path on the western shore of the **Plan d'Amont** to the **Pont de la Sétéria**, 2206m. At the fork in the path beyond go left across the plain to the **Refuge du Fond d'Aussois**, 2324m. Continue northwestwards up to the head of the valley, then steeply up in a northerly direction over glacial striations to the **Col d'Aussois**, 2916m. Tracks lead to the left over boulders to the nearby summit peak of **Pointe de l'Observatoire**, 3015m. Either return the same way or – longer, but nicer – via **Refuge de la Dent Parrachée**, 2511m, one of the mostly beautifully situated huts in the area. To sit there in a deckchair with a refreshing drink enjoying the view makes it worth all the effort.

Summit kiss on the Col d'Aussois.

38 Le Rateau d'Aussois, 3131m

Picturesque circular walk with summit ascent

Plan d'Amont – Col de la Masse – Rateau d'Aussois – Col de la Masse – Refuge de l'Orgère – Col du Barbier

Refuge de l'Orgère with Rateau d'Aussois.

Starting point: Plan d'Amont, 2050m, see Walk 37. Start also possible from the Refuge de l'Orgère, 11km long approach road from St-André to the west of Modane.
Walking times: Plan d'Amont – Col de la Masse 2½ hrs., Col de la Masse – Rateau d'Aussois 1 hr., Rateau d'Aussois – Col de la Masse ½ hr., Col de la Masse – Refuge de l'Orgère 2 hrs., Refuge de l'Orgère – Col du Barbier 2 hrs., Col du Barbier – Plan d'Amont 1½ hrs.; total time 9½ hrs.
Height difference: a good 1500m.
Grade: very long mountain walk where it's best to include an overnight stop in the Refuge de l'Orgère. No paths from the pass to the summit, but marked with cairns. Some snowfields in places in early summer.
Accommodation: Refuge de l'Orgère, CAF, staffed from the end of May to 15. Sept., ✆ 04 79 05 11 65, Refuge de l'Aiguille Doran, staffed 1.6.-15.9., ✆ 06 80 72 46 63.
Map: IGN Top 25, sheet 3534 OT, Les Trois Vallées. Modane.
Tip: if you link Walks 14 and 13 via the Col de la Vanoise with Walk 33, you can extend the route into the Tour des Glacier de la Vanoise (5 to 6 days).

The easily climbed 3000m peak of Rateau offers an excellent view of the Vanoise mountains and the Haute-Maurienne. The largest part of the walk goes along a high trail with few variations in height so that you can concentrate all the more on enjoying the views. A wonderfully scenic gem is the Plateau du Mauvais Berger towards the end of the walk, with lovely pastures between large erratic boulders, with marmots scurrying in between.
From the car park at the dam go up the broad path that, after a sharp bend, runs high above the western shoreline of the **Plan d'Amont**. Before the **Pont de la Sétéria**, 2206m, go to the left steeply up the GR 5 onto a high shelf and continue straight ahead to the west along a zigzag path up onto the **Col de la Masse**, 2923m. Now without paths go in a southerly direction, across a large scree slope between the Petit Rateau lying on the left and the

Rateau d'Aussois lying on the right, afterwards along the ridge to the right to the summit of **Rateau d'Aussois**, 3131m. Return to the **Col de la Masse**, turn westwards and descend round a loop southwards into a cirque. From there the path zigzags southwestwards until at point 2129 the Sentier Nature branches off to the left and runs at first as a beautifully picturesque high trail, then crosses through forest the head of the Orgère valley to the south. At the crossroads and crossing into the wide valley of Maurienne continue left along the GR 5 to the **Col du Barbier**, 2287m. A long traverse after that takes you north across the Plateau du Mauvais Berger high above the two reservoirs. Turn off from the GR in a stream hollow and descend some tracks to the right near the course of the stream (Sentier du ruisseau de la Masse) to the shoreline path and turn right to reach your starting point again.

39 Signal du Petit Mont Cenis, 3162m

Historic peak above Lac du Mont Cenis

Chapelle St-Barthélémy – Col de Sollières – Signal du Petit Mont Cenis and back

Starting point: Chapelle St-Barthélémy, 2012m. Car park at the bridge just beyond. Or 3km further on the Refuge du Petit Mont Cenis, 2110m, see Walk 40.
Walking times: Chapelle St-Barthélémy – Col de Sollières 2 hrs., Col de Sollières – Signal du Petit Mont Cenis 1½ hrs., return 2 hrs.; total time 5½ hrs.
Height difference: 1150m.
Grade: no problems as far as the Col de Sollières. Ridge path is then exposed, sometimes loose scree slopes and unstable boulder fields have to be crossed. Patches of old snow in early summer.
Food and accommodation: on the return via alternative 2) or if the Refuge is chosen as your starting point: Refuge du Petit Mont Cenis, staffed 15. June to 30. Sept., ✆ 04 79 05 88 67.
Alternatives: 1) Adventurous ridge climbing from the Signal du Petit Mont Cenis over the north ridge to Pointe de Cugne, 2984m, 1½ hrs., only suitable for mountain walkers with climbing experience. Descent to the north onto the Col des Randouillards, 2747m, and over the Pas de la Beccia, 2717m, in the east, back to the starting point.
2) Instead of returning the same way: the

Lac du Mont Cenis.

longer way round by 1½ hrs. with even more views goes from the Col de Sollières over the Col des Archettes, 2510m, in the west and over the Col de Bellecombe, 2475m, in the south. Then continue via the alpine mountain huts of Mestrallet to the Col du Petit Mont Cenis, 2183m, and go left along the roadway directly back to the starting point or via the Refuge du Petit Mont Cenis lying south of the roadway.
Map: IGN Top 25, sheet 3634 OT, Val Cenis. Charbonnel.

Sommet historique – a memorial plaque at the highest point of Signal du Petit Mont Cenis celebrates this historic summit. There was a bloody battle between mountain soldiers in April 1945. A peacetime path winds its way across verdant pastures and through bizarrely eroded terrain. The dolines look like bullet holes, but are not. Then the ridge to the summit becomes really exposed, but improves the beautiful view even further. In the east you can see the striking broad pass of Mont Cenis and its large reservoir, in the south, the jagged peaks of the Dents d'Ambin and in the north, the Vanoise glacier and the Dent Parrachée.
From the car park go back along the roadway for a few metres and after the **Chapelle St-Barthélémy**, 2012m, a path branches off left which crosses

the pastureland on a bend to the west parallel to and above the road. Later on you meet the hiking path coming down from the Refuge du Petit Mont Cenis. At the fork in the path, 2246m, just beyond it, you can go either left or right. Both routes join up again on a terrace higher up. First go across some bizarrely eroded terrain, then over undulating meadows to the north onto the **Col de Sollières**, 2639m. Continue east along some tracks to the start of the ridge. First right, then left follow the line of the ridge onto a small col. Continue left along the ridge steeply up to the summit of **Signal du Petit Mont Cenis**, 3162m.

Return the same way.

40 Lac de Savine, 2447m – Lacs Giaset, 2664m

Hannibal once passed through here

Refuge du Petit Mont Cenis – Lacs Perrin – Lac de Savine – Lacs Giaset – Lacs Perrin – Refuge du Petit Mont Cenis

Information board at the Refuge du Petit Mont Cenis.

Starting point: Refuge du Petit Mont Cenis, 2110m, drive from the Col du Mont Cenis, 2081m, along a small 6½km long road or it's 1¾ hrs. on foot.
Walking times: Refuge du Petit Mont Cenis – Lacs Perrin ¾ hr., Lacs Perrin – Lac de Savine 1¾ hr; Lac de Savine – Lacs Giaset a good ¾ hr., Lacs Giaset – Refuge du Petit Mont Cenis just under 1¾ hrs.; total time 5 hrs.
Height difference: 700m.
Grade: alpine ascent from Lac de Savine to Lacs Giaset, the adjoining traverse to Lacs Perrin is also really exposed, sure-footedness is important here. A walk suitable for families as far as Lac de Savine or another ½ hr. further on to the Col Clapier.
Food and accommodation: Refuge du Petit Mont Cenis, staffed 15. June to 30. Sept., ✆ 04 79 05 88 67.
Alternative: rewarding traverse from the Col Clapier via the Col de l'Agnel to the Refuge d'Ambin, 5½ hrs. 4 hrs. back the next day to the Refuge du Petit Mont Cenis.
Map: IGN Top 25, sheet 3634 OT, Val Cenis. Charbonnel.

Hannibal is supposed to have travelled over the Col Clapier in 218 BC to make a surprise attack on Rome by coming across the Alps. Perhaps his large army and his elephants made camp on Lac de Savine – a legend which adds a special nuance to this beautiful walk, any how. The delightful starting point of the Refuge du Petit Mont Cenis was a former stable which today spoils its guests with local cuisine. From the idyllic valley floor the walk then continues through the rugged beauty of the Vallon de Savine onto a wonderful terrace of land covered with lakes. The view of the jagged peaks of the Dents d'Ambin is particularly spectacular.

At the garden terrace of the **Refuge du Petit Mont Cenis** an info board provides you with useful information (the yellow marked paths around the refuge were created through an independent initiative and are not to be found on any of the IGN maps). First take the path to the west at the edge of the flat valley floor, then southwards across grassy hillsides onto the terrace of land with **Lacs Perrin**, 2372m. Continue through the small high valley running southwards onto a small col and down over a steep shelf into the Vallon de

Savine. A steady and unremitting broad path runs upstream to the **Lac de Savine**, 2447m.

Just before the lake follow the yellow marked path to the left. This path leads across boulder fields and broken rock onto a pass, 2972m, on the northwest ridge of Mont Giusalet. The cairns guide you across the stony plateau with **Lacs Giaset**, 2664m, at first to the north, then northwestwards. Cross the exposed ledges below Pointe Droset into the high valley of **Lacs Perrin** again and return the same way to the **refuge**.

41 Vallon d'Ambin – Pas de la Coche, 2968m

Unparalleled high mountain scenery

Le Planay – Refuge d'Ambin – Pas de la Coche – Plan des Eaux – Chapelle de St-Barthélémy – Le Planay

Starting point: Le Planay, 1660m, car park at the bridge over Ruisseau d'Etache opposite the Lavis-Trafford chalet. Approach from the N 6 at Bramans along the D 100.

Walking times: Le Planay – Refuge d'Ambin 2¼ hrs., Refuge d'Ambin – Pas de la Coche 2½ hrs., Pas de la Coche – Plan des Eaux 1 hr., Plan des Eaux – Le Planay 2 hrs.; total time 7¾ hrs.

Height difference: 1320m.

Grade: demanding mountain walk that requires sure-footedness and a certain level of fitness. At the Pas de la Coche sometimes without paths over boulder fields. From the Plan d'Etache you have to negotiate a steep moraine where the path can often be intermittent due to landslides. There are still patches of old snow in places at the beginning of July.

Food and accommodation: Refuge d'Ambin, staffed end of June to 15. Sept., ✆ 04 79 20 35 00; Le Planay: Chambres d'hôtes Chalet Lavis Trafford, ✆ 04 79 05 06 83; Refuge-Auberge La Tourna, ✆ 04 79 05 23 29; Refuge du Suffet, ✆ 04 79 05 30 17.

Alternative: a separate walk or a marvellous extension to the walk (which then makes it into a very long day) is the high trail above the Vallon d'Etache to Lac du Liael. From the Plan des Eaux first go towards the Col de Bramanette, then cross below the pass along the high shelf northwards to the Lac du Liael, 2550m, (2 hrs.); Lac du Liael – eastern ridge of Pointe du Clôt – Chalets de Montbas – Le Planay 2 hrs.

Map: IGN Top 25, sheet 3634 OT, Val Cenis. Charbonnel. Better, with more paths marked: IGN Alpes sans Frontières, sheet 12.

Tips: the church of St-Pierre d'Extravache dating from the 10th century at the start of Val d'Ambin is the oldest in Savoy.

Numerous summit ascents can be found in the topo guide, Alpinisme Vanoise Haute-Maurienne, by Patrick Col, only in French, obtainable from local bookshops.

While the Vanoise National Park is extensively marketed and its main paths are well used in the summer months, the Val d'Ambin lying opposite is still a secret oasis. Some very moderate tourism has arrived today after centuries of seclusion with charming accommodation, but otherwise nothing except remote and exciting nature which can be explored along a perfectly marked network of paths which extends across the border. Four elongated high valleys, those of Bramanette, Etache, Ambin and Savine, allow access and views into the over 3000m high border ridge with Italy. The walk through the Vallon d'Ambin via the Pas de la Coche into the Vallon d'Etache is the quintessence of wild mountain scenery full of clear mountain lakes, glaciated hillsides, rocky crags and idyllic areas of meadow.

From **Le Planay** continue along the roadway to the east up the Vallon d'Ambin. The Maroqua car park at the end of the road, 1985m, is reached after 4km. A stony path sets off along the right hand bank to the **Refuge d'Ambin**, 2270m, situated on a high shelf. Go past the hut to the fork. Go

Fabulous views of Grand Cordonnier on the ascent up to Lac Noir.

right across the bridge and the path zigzags up onto a small plateau, 2650m, with good views and a fork with two alternatives that head for the same destination. Whether you go left or right, you are standing on the long rocky terrace of **Lac Noir**, 2800m, about 50 minutes later. From its southern end go northwestwards over boulders and scree to the **Pas de la Coche**, 2968m, which reveals a wonderful view northwards to the Dent Parrachée. From the col go west without paths (but well marked) over boulders, then across pastures onto the meadow of **Plan d'Etache**, 2775m, to the tiny southernmost lake, 2738m. Cross the stream and on the other side go in a northerly direction down a steep wall of moraine. Continue a little way along the right hand bank, then change again onto the left bank and up to the pool of **Plan d'Eaux**, 2495m, below the dolomitic-type rock walls of Grand Bec d'Etache. Go across the meadows strewn with boulders towards the western stream channel and on the other side to the Ruisseau de Côte Cornue. Descend its steep left hand bank into the bottom of the Vallon d'Etache. Continue along the right hand side of the valley, past the **Chapelle de St-Barthélémy**, 2010m, back to **Le Planay**.

Idyllic place to stop for a picnic below Grand Bec d'Etache.

42 Mont Thabor, 3178m

A pilgrimage mountain with divinely created scenery

Le Lavoir – Col de la Vallée Etroite – Lac du Peyron – Col des Méandes – Mont Thabor – Refuge du Mont Thabor – Le Lavoir

Starting point: Le Lavoir, 1923m, car park directly after the Fort du Lavoir. Approach from Modane to Valfréjus. Behind the ski station turn off to the right, 3½km gravel track.

Walking times: Le Lavoir – Col de la Vallée Etroite 2 hrs., Col de la Vallée Etroite – Lac du Peyron 1 hr., Lac du Peyron – Mont Thabor 2½ hrs., Mont Thabor – Col de la Vallée Etroite 2 hrs., Col de la Vallée Etroite – Refuge du Mont Thabor ¼ hr., Refuge du Mont Thabor – Le Lavoir 1¾ hrs.; total time 9½ hrs.

Height difference: 1400m.

Grade: long mountain walk with large variation in height, a few sections are really steep and slippery on the descent. It's advisable to stay overnight in the refuge. Be prepared for patches of old snow in early summer.

Food and accommodation: Refuge du Mont Thabor, CAF, staffed middle of June to middle of Sept.; ✆ 04 79 20 32 13.

Map: IGN Top 25, sheet 3535 OT, Névache. Mont Thabor.

Tip: the Tour du Mont Thabor is highly recommended which takes 6 days to go round Mont Thabor and ascend the summit (suggested book: Autour du Thabor, Glénat Verlag). If you only have 2 or 3 days time: Refuge du Mont Thabor – Col du Cheval Blanc – Passage du Pic du Thabor – Col de Névache – Refuge des Drayères (✆ 04 92 21 36 01) 6 hrs.; Refuge des Drayères – Col des Méandes – Roche de Chardonnet – Col de Valmeinier – Mont Thabor – Col de la Vallée Etroite – Refuge du Mont Thabor 6 hrs.

View from Mont Thabor to Italy into the Vallée Etroite.

Ascent to the Refuge Mont Thabor.

Is it the ochre-coloured desert landscape of the majestic Mont Thabor which causes everyday cares to evaporate and gives you the space for tranquility and reflection? Or because the whole world lies splendidly at your feet with the view reaching from Mont Blanc to Mont Viso, because marvellous lakes glisten in the depths between dark pinnacles and delightful alpine pastures lie embedded in the Vallée Clarée? Or could it be that you simply feel very close to your maker when you are up so high? The fact of the matter is that many pilgrims are attracted to the pilgrimage chapel on the summit all year round, especially on the Sunday after 15. August when the big annual pilgrimage takes place with a mass at an altitude of over 3000m. The origin of this pilgrimage is a typhoid epidemic which struck the region in 1860 and claimed many lives. From then on the inhabitants of the surrounding valleys have climbed the mountain to entreat the Madonna of Thabor for protection. The origins of the chapel itself remain a mystery and are wreathed in many legends.

On the shore of Lac du Peyron.

From **Le Lavoir** car park go up beside the Ruisseau du Charmaix along the roadway to the fork at a small weir. Continue left along the GR 5 on the same side of the valley across sloping meadows to the south. The striking rock plinth of Cheval Blanc and the Refuge du Mont Thabor lying in a solitary location below, always remain in sight. Behind the large wooden cross of the **Col de la Vallée Etroite**, 2434m, cross over to the right westwards into the Vallon de la Dame, then loop round into the Vallon du Peyron and onto the southern terrace with **Lac du Peyron**, 2453m. Past its northern shore ascend steeply to the south around a rock barrier and along the ridge of rock onto the **Col des Méandes**, 2727m, situated to the west. Descend gently right to the foot of the ochre-coloured mountain, le Pied du Désert. After crossing a stream go steeply up the exposed scree path and onto the start of the ridge with a cross which marks the beginning of the pilgrimage path that is lined with many crosses. The route snakes across the broad

eastern face of Mont Thabor, reaches the pilgrimage chapel, 3130m, and runs a bit further along the ridge southwestwards to the highest point of **Mont Thabor**, 3178m.

Return as far as the Col de la Vallée Etroite. Turn left there to the **Refuge du Mont Thabor**, 2502m. It's worth taking a detour to the lakes of Lac Rond and Lac Long close to the hut. For the return take the yellow and red marked path from the hut northwards. Now go along the other side of the valley via the **Chalets du Mounioz**, 2386m, to the bridge at the small weir where you meet the ascent route again. Turn left down the roadway to the car park.

43 Tour de la Fourche

4 lake walk below Galibier

Plan Lachat – Lac des Cerces – Col des Cerces – Lac Rond – Lac du Grand Ban – Col des Rochilles – Camp des Rochilles – Plan Lachat

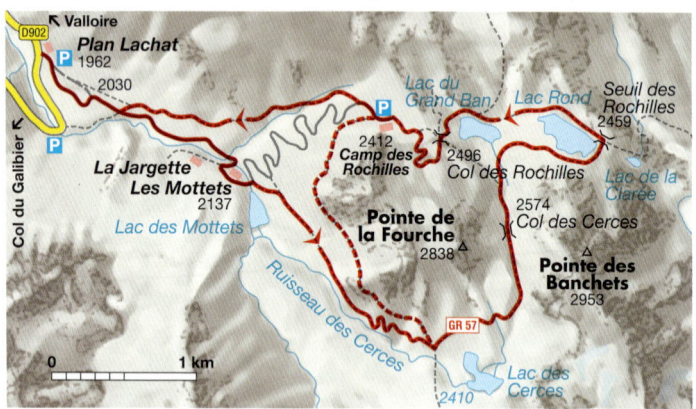

Starting point: Plan Lachat, 1962m, turn-off left along a gravel track just before the sharp right hand bend at the head of the valley, 10km from Valloire in the direction of Col du Galibier.
Walking times: Plan Lachat – Lac des Cerces 1¾ hrs., Lac des Cerces – Lac Rond 1¼ hrs., Lac Rond – Camp des Rochilles ¾ hr., Camp des Rochilles – Plan Lachat ¾ hr.;
total time 4½ hrs.
Height difference: 612m.

Grade: easy mountain walk, ideal walk for families, short section by Lac Rond across boulders.
Food: none.
Alternative: the Camp des Rochilles is also accessible by car along a 5km long, rough gravel track. If you start from there – and climb directly up to the Lac des Cerces – the walk takes 1 hr. less.
Map: IGN Top 25, sheet 3435 ET, Valloire. Aiguilles d'Arves. Col du Galibier; or sheet 3535 OT Névache. Mont Thabor.

The road over the Col du Galibier that links the Maurienne with the Briançonnais is one of the most well-known sections of the legendary 'Grande Route des Alpes', the high trail through the French Alps. It is especially famous because the Tour de France has often raced through here. The route climbs out of Val d'Arc round innumerable bends at first over the Col du Télégraphe into the Vallée de Valloirette with the popular winter sports centre of Valloire, then winds its way through wonderful high mountain scenery towards the rock wastes of the Col du Galibier. Again and again you catch glimpses of idyllic small high valleys which arouse your curiosity and inspire you to take a further look. At the head of the Vallée de Valloirette you are afforded magnificent views of Grand Galibier, as well as the hidden lakes on the pass over to the Vallée Clarée. You also drive round the Pointe de la Fourche massif on the way.

From **Plan Lachat**, 1962m, follow the gravel track as far as the alpine mountain huts of **Les Mottets**, 2137m. On the left hand bend afterwards the hiking path branches off to the right that crosses the meadows to the Ruisseau des Cerces and, close to the bank, goes uphill to the plateau with the **Lac des Cerces**, 2410m. At the fork beforehand continue along the white, red and white marked GR 57 at first eastwards, then northwards below the walls of Pointe de la Fourche onto the **Col des Cerces**, 2574m.

From the pass go through the little valley, leave the turn-off to the Col des Rochilles on the left and descend to the plain of the lakes where you cross over right to the south bank of Lac Rond and continue, at times over boulders, onto the col, the **Seuil des Rochilles**, 2459m. Lac de la Clarée, 2433m, shimmers green a little below you in the east. Carry on to the left along a comfortable footpath along the northern banks of **Lac Rond** and **Lac du Grand Ban** onto the **Col des Rochilles**, 2496m. Go downhill to the military buildings of Camp des Rochilles, 2412m, where a hiking path soon turns off right from the track taking a shortcut from the many loops in the road and leads you back to the **Plan Lachat**.

View down to the Camp des Rochilles.

133

44 Col des Aiguilles d'Arves, 3163m

Close examination of the Aiguilles d'Arves

Bonnenuit – Refuge des Aiguilles d'Arves – Col des Aiguilles d'Arves and back

Col des Aiguilles d'Arves with Tête de Chat.

Starting point: Hameau de Bonnenuit, a hamlet 6km from Valloire. Car park, 1666m, on the right of the road to the Col du Galibier.
Walking times: car park – Refuge des Aiguilles d'Arves 2 hrs., refuge – Col des Aiguilles d'Arves 2½ hrs., return 3½ hrs.; total time 8 hrs.
Height difference: 1500m.
Grade: strenuous mountain walk with a large variation in height, unstable scree slopes and boulder fields in the upper area. Sure-footedness, a sense of direction and a good level of fitness very important! It's advisable, in any case, to stay overnight in the refuge since the Aiguilles are often enveloped in clouds from midday.
Food and accommodation: Refuge des Aiguilles d'Arves, CAF, staffed beginning of June until middle of September, ✆ 04 79 59 01 77; Gîte d'Etape Les Réaux in Bonnenuit, ✆ 04 79 59 06 64.
Alternatives: 1) The Aiguille de l'Epaisseur, 3230m is a wonderful belvedere over the Aiguilles and much easier to climb. Take the ascending path to the right after the refuge, 3 hrs. 2) Only for mountain walkers with climbing experience, the Tête de Chat – it reminds you of a cat's head with its two 'ears' – is the easiest of the three Aiguilles to climb. From the Col des Aiguilles d'Arves follow the cairns, from the col to the right to a conspicuous rock tower. Go through the chimney, then cross right along a ledge, zigzag up over various ledges across the east face, then onto the south face. Crux (III, safety bolts), a short distance over uneven rock to the summit of the southern 'ear'; 45 mins. Exact route descriptions of all three towers available in the refuge or in the Bureau des Guides in Valloire ✆ 04 79 83 35 03.
Map: IGN Top 25, sheet 3435, Valloire. Aiguilles d'Arves. Col du Galibier.

Although situated directly at the *départment* border with the Dauphiné, the Aiguilles d'Arves are referred to as the mountain symbol for the Maurienne. The gigantic plinth with the three elegant rock pyramids separates the Savoy valleys of Valloire (east) and Arves (west). Enthusiasts refer to it as the most beautiful trinity of the Alps. It is the major aim of local residents to have stood on top.

But for that you need mountaineering equipment and experience. However a sure-footed, fit mountain walker can get as far as the col between the Aiguille Centrale and the Tête de Chat. A view from there down into the dizzying depths or of the steep rock faces of the sheer pinnacles more than compensates for the tough ascent.

From the car park descend right to the wooden bridge and cross the Valloirette. Go left through a larch wood with a short steep ascent to the alpine mountain huts of **Les Aiguilles**, 1845m. Continue west up a more moderate incline along the left hand side of the Torrent des Aiguilles to the **Refuge des Aiguilles d'Arves**, 2260m. Go past the hut through the Combe des Aiguilles, then steeply northwards towards the ridge to a conspicuous rock shelf half way along. Do not go straight ahead, continue left in a westerly direction. Zigzag up across scree, then over boulders to the miserable remains of the Glacier des Aiguilles d'Arves. Cross the glacier (not dangerous, but slippery) and onto the **Col des Aiguilles d'Arves**, 3163m, between the Aiguille Centrale and the Tête de Chat. Return the same way.

135

45 Basse du Gerbier, 2578m

Viewing terrace at the foot of the Aiguilles d'Arves

Chalmieu – Relais TV – Basse du Gerbier and back

Starting point: Relais TV (transmitting station), 1910m.
Drive along the D 926 from the Arvan valley, then onto the D 80 in the direction of Albiez, after about 1km turn right onto the D 80A via Montrond to Chalmieu and continue to the end of the tarmac road.
Walking times: Relais TV – Basse du Gerbier 2¼ hrs., return 1¼ hrs.; total time 3½ hrs.

Height difference: 670m.
Grade: easy mountain walk on good paths, although muddy when wet.
Food and accommodation: Gîte d'Etape Clairevie, St-Sorlin d'Arves, ✆ 04 79 59 71 26, e-mail eric.axelrad@wanadoo.fr. Gîte d'Etape in La Villette, hamlet below Albiez, ✆ / Fax 04 79 59 38 03, e-mail GAUTHE@net-up.com.
Map: IGN Top 25, sheet 3435, Valloire. Aiguilles d'Arves. Col du Galibier.

You can see them from many of the summits, valleys and passes in Savoy – the elegant three spikes of the Aiguilles d'Arves which are reminiscent of the three pinnacles of the Dolomites. And in just the same way, hordes of moun-

The Aiguilles d'Arves with the horses on the meadows of the Basse du Gerbier.

tain walkers traipse up to the striking symbol of the Maurienne.

They are at their best seen from the Arvan valley. They soar up in breathtaking beauty from the wide prairies of the verdant hills. You come closest to their vertical faces at the Basse du Gerbier. The picturesque terraced meadows complete the panorama with a fantastic distant view to the north – on the left of the high terrace of Albiez you can see Mont Charvin with its bizarre

The Aiguilles d'Arves are usually enveloped in cloud in the afternoon.

rock chimneys and Mont Blanc glistens on the far horizon. The barren region was once covered with forest. You can still see a few individual petrified trees in the hollow at the foot of Gros Crey.

From the **transmitting station** follow the roadway. It soon turns into a path and winds along the eastern edge of the broad hollow of Outre l'Eau which is bordered in the west by the conspicuous grassy ridge of Crête de Chenallin. Continue up and down over grassy hills and several streams to the south.

A little way above the alpine mountain hut of **La Motte**, 2179m, the path veers to the west, crosses the side streams and the Ruisseau de l'Olletaz and curves across the grassy terrain onto the meadows of the **Basse du Gerbier**, 2578m.

Return the same way.

46 Cime de la Valette, 2858m

Bizarre verdant mountains

Les Deux Ponts – Col des Prés Nouveaux – Col de la Valette – Cime de la Valette – Les Arènes – Le Laital – Pré Bernard – Les Deux Ponts

Starting point: Les Deux Ponts, 1596m, beyond the hamlet of Les Prés Plans in the valley of Torrent l'Arvan, 4km from St-Sorlin d'Arves, 1510m. Possible to park after the first bridge.
Walking times: Les Deux Ponts – Pravel 1 hr., Pravel – Col des Prés Nouveaux 2½ hrs., Col des Prés Nouveaux – Col de la Valette ¾ hr., Col de la Valette – Cime de la Valette 1¾ hrs., Cime de la Valette – Les Aigues Rousses 1¼ hrs., Les Aigues Rousses – Les Deux Ponts ½ hr.; total time 8¾ hrs.
Height difference: 1300m.
Grade: very long day walk for fit hikers. On the return, several cattle paths might proove confusing, so having a sense of direction is an advantage.
Food: none.

Accommodation: Gîte d'Etape Clairevie, St-Sorlin d'Arves, ✆ 04 79 59 71 26, e-mail eric.axelrad@wanadoo.fr.
Alternative: from the Col de la Valette via the Lac des Quirlies and the Crête des Sauvages to the Cime de la Valette: demanding 2 day walk with an overnight camp at Lac des Quirlies, only for adventurous, sure-footed mountain walkers with a good sense of direction, the crossing from Lac des Quirlies to the Cime de la Valette sometimes goes without paths over broken rock; Les Deux Ponts – Col de la Valette – Lac des Quirlies 6¼ hrs., Lac des Quierlies – Cime de la Valette – Les Deux Ponts 5½ hrs., height difference 1600m.
Map: IGN Top 25, sheet 3335 ET, Le Bourg d'Oisans. L'Alpe d'Huez.

The Crête des Sauvages is inhabited by hundreds of sheep.

The pretty Chapelle de Pré Plan on the way to Les Deux Ponts.

A bumpy gravel road goes from the holiday resort of St-Sorlin d'Arves, past the ancient hamlet of Pré-Plan, into the remote Arvan valley. From then on it only goes along remote paths. The route to the Col des Prés Nouveaux is accompanied by a quite curious-looking landscape. Green verdant mountains, dramatically divided by brilliant violet slate gullies, tower up on all sides into the sky. From the grassy ridge which comes up from the pass to the Cime de la Valette, you can enjoy a spectacular array of peaks – Mont Blanc in the north, the sheer jagged peaks of the Ecrin massif in the south. The Glacier des Quirlies glistens close by as it sweeps down from the south face of Pic de l'Etendard. If you have a good sense of direction and also a tent with you, there awaits another highlight somewhere up there amongst the moraine debris – the Lac des Quierlies, one of the last alpine lakes into which a glacier is still carving its way. The future of this natural spectacle seems to be more and more threatened by the ever-increasing melting of the glacier. The approach from the Arvan valley is rarely walked. The only forms of life that you meet as you cross from the ridge to the lake are sheep. Hordes of bleating balls of wool graze the verdant hills and broad plateaus – a picture you might have expected in New Zealand, but not in the French Alps.

From **Les Deux Ponts**, 1596m, follow the track to the left and go left again after the second bridge. The track soon turns into a path, gradually ascends through woods and meadows and then runs over open pastureland along the eastern side of the Torrent l'Arvettaz via the alpine mountain huts of **Pravel**, 1825m, to the **Col des Prés Nouveaux**, 2292m. An old border stone (French Borne) from the time when Savoy did not belong to France, marks the broad grassy hollow of the pass. The symbol of the royal lily of France shines resplendently on its southern side, the cross of Savoy on the north side. The view of the glaciated Ecrins massif in the south is simply stunning while in the north, Mont Blanc and the Vanoise peaks with Grande Casse come into view. From the border stone follow the grassy path to the right onto the high ridge and cross below the south side of the ridge to the **Col de la Valette**, 2291m. From here go along the ridge easily northwestwards to the **Cime de la Valette**, 2858m, where wonderful views of the glaciers of Pic de l'Etendard await you.

From the summit follow the northeast ridge of **Les Arènes** to a small col. Turn right there to the small lake of **Le Laital**, 2469m. Even though from here the route is marked with yellow painted posts, you need to take great care as the numerous cattle paths can be confusing. Past the alpine mountain hut of **Les Aigues Rousses** continue steeply up round zigzags to the east, then on a long traverse to the north above the deep valley cleft to the alpine mountain huts of **Pré Bernard**. The last leisurely section is along a track back to the starting point at **Les Deux Ponts**.

Lac des Quirlies with Glacier Quirlies in the golden light of evening.

47 Glacier de St-Sorlin, 2715m

Parade of lakes and glacier spectacle on Pic de l'Etendard

Col de la Croix de Fer – Refuge de l'Etendard – Glacier de St-Sorlin – Lac Bramant – Col Nord des Lacs – Col de la Croix de Fer

Starting point: Col de la Croix de Fer, 2067m, large car park.
A 43, either Sortie 27 St-Jean-de-Maurienne and D 926 via St-Sorlin or Sortie St-Marie-de-Cuines and D 927 through Vallée des Villards.
Walking times: Col de la Croix de Fer – Refuge de l'Etendard 2 hrs., Refuge de l'Etendard – Glacier de St-Sorlin 1¾ hrs., Glacier de St-Sorlin – Col Nord des Lacs 1½ hrs., Col Nord des Lacs – Col de la Croix de Fer 1¼ hrs.; total time 6½ hrs.
Height difference: about 800m.
Grade: easy mountain walk with a few steep sections.
Food: Chalet de la Croix de Fer on the pass of the same name; Refuge de l'Etendard.
Accommodation: Refuge de l'Etendard, staffed 20. June to 15. Sept., ✆ 04 79 59 74 96.
Alternative: the ascent of Pic de l'Etendard (4 hrs. from the Refuge) is a rewarding classic and is classified as an easy glacier path. Only undertake with a complete set of mountain equipment (rope, crampons, ice axe) and glacier experience, advisable to use a mountain guide (Bureau des Guides de Montagne, ✆ 04 79 59 74 06).
Map: IGN Top 25, sheet 3335 ET, Le Bourg d'Oisans. L'Alpe d'Huez.

The Glacier de St-Sorlin in the first rays of the sun.

143

Regular crowds of hikers traipse up to the hut on sunny weekends and towards Pic de l'Etendard – some in full glacier gear with heavy rucksacks, others dressed for a stroll up to the pretty lakes, often with children in tow, many with complete camping gear on their backs. Everyone meets up at the Refuge de l'Etendard. The hut warden, Bruno Axelrad, half Austrian, has taken over the rustic accommodation once run by his mother. In those days the hut was well known for 'l'Autrichienne' who could make excellent apple strudels and goulash. And that is still on the menu today. You can really find that it slows your pulse as you walk round the lake – a cool swim, a spot of sunbathing or a picnic on the soft shoreline meadows, admire the reflection of the mountains in the water, especially the reflection of the beautiful sheer pinnacles of the Aiguilles de l'Argentière in the Lac Bramant. It's really worthwhile getting up very early with others who are heading for the summit and follow the dancing line of the lights

An array of peaks across the Vanoise National Park with La Grande Casse.

Le Laitelet on the Col de la Croix de Fer.

from their torches up to the tongue of the glacier. Only then can you experience an extraordinary scene which takes your breath away. The first rays of the sun breathe fire into the glacier – out of this world! The section between the glacier and the lakes affords a view of Mont Blanc and the Vanoise peaks.

From the **Col de la Croix de Fer** descend the track opposite the chalet for a few metres to the fork and follow it right in a westerly direction. The track then turns southwards into a high valley and goes round many bends on the western face of Les Perrons onto a small high terrace, then down to the now visible **Refuge de l'Etendard**, 2430m. Go along the western shore of the lakes, Lac Bramant and Lac Blanc. After the second lake the path changes over onto the other side of the valley. Continue southwards through the moraine landscape to the start of the tongue of the **Glacier de St-Sorlin**, 2715m.

Return to the fork before Lac Blanc. Now turn to the right along the eastern shore of the lakes until, about half way along Lac Bramant, a path ascends to the right to the **Col Nord des Lacs**, 2533m. Descend the col eastwards and loop round across a scarred skiing area northwards below the eastern precipices of Les Perrons back to the **Col de la Croix de Fer**.

48 Lac de la Croix, 2415m – Col du Sambuis, 2528m

Wild mountain country on the Col du Glandon

Col du Glandon – Lac de la Croix – Col du Sambuis – Lac du Sambuis – Plan des Trois Eaux – Col du Glandon

Starting point: Col du Glandon, 1924m, car park and info board. Drive from the Maurienne via the A 43, Sortie St-Marie-de-Cuines, then along the D 927 through the Vallée des Villards. Or from the Arvan valley via the Col de la Croix de Fer.
Walking times: Col du Glandon – Lac de la Croix 2 hrs., Lac de la Croix – Plan des Trois Eaux 2 hrs., Plan des Trois Eaux – Col du Glandon 1 hr.; total time 5 hrs.
Height difference: a good 600m.
Grade: easy walk there except for a short exposed section through a notch at the head of the valley after Plan des Trois Eaux. Pathless section over the Col du Sambuis to the Lac du Sambuis and only sparingly marked with cairns, demands a good sense of direction and sure-footedness. Only to be undertaken in clear visibility.
Alternative: the Cime du Sambuis, 2727m, a very beautiful viewing peak. Approach at the start of the Combe de la Croixon to the right and follow the cairns, ascent from the pass 3 hrs.
Map: IGN Top 25, sheet 3335 ET, Le Bourg d'Oisans. L'Alpe d'Huez.

Cycling enthusiasts are well acquainted with the Vallée des Villards in the Belledonne north massif that runs up round sweat-generating bends through marvellous undeveloped scenery to the Col du Glandon. The nearer you get to the pass, the more impressively the sheer pinnacles of the

146

On the Col du Glandon.

Aiguilles de l'Argentière penetrate up into the sky. The Col du Glandon allows you access into a hidden high valley that affords even more stunning views of the sheer peaks and idyllic small terraces with lakes are to be found along the path.

From the **Col du Glandon** go west along the path below the alpine mountain huts gently downhill through bushes into a stream channel, then across below the eastern corner buttress of the Aiguilles de l'Argentière into the **Combe de la Croix**. It's a moderate incline on the left of the stream, at times over boulders, to the head of the valley, **Plan des Trois Eaux**, 2134m. Go across three tiny streams towards the notch lying slightly on the right which requires some easy climbing. You come to a cirque where, right at the start, you cross the stream over to the right. Follow the cairns up a steep zigzag path onto the plateau with the **Lac de la Croix**, 2415m. Continue along feint tracks at the eastern end of the lake towards the conspicuous round knoll. Ascend to the left of it through boulders to the **Col du Sambuis**, 2528m. You can see two tiny lakes. From the lower one there are only a very few cairns to guide you eastwards over boulders through a gully to the **Lac du Sambuis**, 2432m, where, just afterwards, you meet the now well marked path up to the Cime du Sambuis. Descend southwards along this path into the Combe de la Croix, cross the bridge and return to the **Col du Glandon** back along the way you came.

49 Mont Rond d'en bas, 1522m

Viewing point for walkers and via ferrata enthusiasts

Valmaure – Combe du Tépey – Mont Rond d'en bas – Descente du Réposeu – La Chal – Valmaure

Starting point: Valmaure, 1205m, car park at the village well. Approach turns off right after St-Colomban via Les Roches.
Walking times: Valmaure – Mont Rond d'en bas 1 hr., Mont Rond d'en bas – Valmaure 1 hr.; total time 2 hrs.
Height difference: 330m.
Grade: easy mountain walk with steep descent down the Descente du Réposeu, ideal walk with families or escape route for via ferrata enthusiasts.
Food: none.
Accommodation: Auberge du Glandon, ✆ 04 79 56 25 16 and Hôtel de la Poste, ✆ 04 79 56 25 33, in St-Colomban-des-Villards; both very basic, but good value for money.
Map: IGN Top 25, sheet 3433 OT Allevard. Belledonne Nord (out of print at present).
Tip: a demanding via ferrata with suspension and cable bridges goes across the rocky east face of Mont Rond d'en bas. Car park for the de la Chal via ferrata at the bridge after the hamlet of La Chal, 1208m. Info board and also practice route for beginners and children. Path at the start – via ferrata 2½ hrs.; descent from Mont Rond d'en bas via the 'Descente du Réposeu' ½ hr., in total 3 hrs.

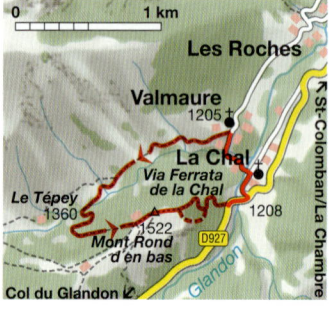

The hill of Mont Rond d'en bas is the perfect belvedere from which to have a view along the whole length of the Villards valley – spectacular via ferrata crags on one side, an idyllic mixed forest of moss and ferns on the other, a meadow of beautiful flowers on the top of the hill and enchanting hamlets at its feet.

From the well take the path ascending on the right through the houses. This pretty lane then goes steeply up towards the Vallon du Tépey. At the fork descend slightly to the left via the Combe du Tépey to the delightful stream and cross over the **Passerelle du Tépey**, 1360m. After the bridge ascend right up through the forest to the clearing with the chalets of **Mont Rond d'en bas**, 1522m, where you reach the top. A detour along the grassy ridge to the right affords you beautiful views into the barren Vallon du Tépey and the upper Villards valley. Go left after the first chalet, without paths down the sloping meadow along the edge of the forest until you come to the signpost for the via ferrata descent route. The 'Descente du Réposeu' winds steeply down the rocky slope of the forest into the bottom of the valley. Right at the start of the forest there's a rock which provides you with fantastic views of the elongated valley and Mont Blanc in the distant mist. Be careful to continue left from the rock, do not turn right. Some of the tracks are a bit confusing and can lead you the wrong way. You finally come out at the via ferrata car park. Now it's just a few metres along the road. Go over the bridge and turn left between the group of houses of **La Chal**, 1208m. The first tarmac road to the left takes you back to **Valmaure**.

The de la Chal via ferrata is a pretty alternative on Mont Rond d'en bas.

50 Pic de Fremezan, 2261m

Exposed summit ridge and lake high above the Villards valley

St-Colomban-des-Villards – Planard de Combe Rousse – Pic de Fremezan – Lac des Balmettes – St-Colomban-des-Villards

Starting point: end of the forest road 'La route O.N.F. de Fremezan', stone house with barbecue site, 1828m, 8km from St-Colomban-des-Villards, 1102m. Drive (coming from Maurienne) to the right before the church.
Walking times: car park – point 2207 2 hrs., point 2207 – Pic de Fremezan 1¼ hrs., Pic de Fremezan – Lac des Balmettes 1 hr., Lac des Balmettes – car park ¾ hr.; total time 5 hrs.
Height difference: 450m.
Grade: the descent to Lac des Balmettes and the ridge path to Pic de Fremezan are very exposed and demand sure-footedness. A good sense of direction is essential as there are few signposts. Patches of old snow in early summer.
Food: none.
Accommodation: Auberge du Glandon, ✆ 04 79 56 25 16 and Hôtel de la Poste, ✆ 04 79 56 25 33, in St-Colomban-des-Villards; both of them very basic, but good value for money.
Alternative: a very beautiful summit ascent, but which requires sure-footedness, a level of fitness and a good sense of direction, goes from Lac des Balmettes over the Col des Balmettes to the Col du Villonet (approach also possible from the Planard de Combe Rousse through the Combe Rousse). Continue to the west through a cirque, then very steeply up a scree slope into the Brèches de la Passoire. Go along the ridge to the south with some easy climbing onto the summit of Pointe de l'Aup du Pont, 2713m. 2½ hrs. there and back from Lac des Balmettes.
Map: IGN Top 25, sheet 3433 OT Allevard. Belledonne Nord (out of print at present).

High above the Vallée des Villards.

The idyllic Vallée des Villards is for the most part covered in forest together with small and pretty villages in the back of beyond where, apart from the small amount of traffic on the pass, the game of boules is the main attraction in village life. And if you cannot see anything beyond the trees, then you are strongly advised to hike along the upper level where the forest no longer stands a chance of surviving and discover open views of the wild mountain landscape and a breathtaking array of peaks from Mont Blanc to the Ecrins.

Follow the path from the end of the forest road, 1828m, which first zigzags in between avalanche barriers into the mountains. Just before the last barriers go straight ahead on a right hand bend and cross the slope to the west below the southern face of Pic de Fremezan. Go below an area of boulders into a hollow, then around a mountain ridge, 2103m, or directly onto it from the hollow. Continue to ascend the small high valley of **Planard de Combe Rousse** in a westerly direction to a small col. From there descend easily and cross over to **point 2207**. A wooden sign indicates right to the Pic de Fremezan. Go uphill across grassy hillsides along feint tracks to the northeast up to the col, 2432m, on the western ridge of Pic de Fremezan. An exposed little path goes on the right below the ridge in an easterly direction to **Pic de Fremezan**, 2261m. Return the same way from the summit onto the col and descend steeply on its north side to **Lac des Balmettes**, 2196m. Continue to descend along the yellow and red marked GRP Arvan-Villards on the left of the Doron des Croix stream. At a fork leave the GRP to the right and shortly afterwards turn off again to the right to the stream. Cross the stream over to the avalanche barriers and back to the car park.

51 Grand Coin, 2730m

Spectacular ridge walk

Col du Chaussy – Fontaine Bénite – Crêt Lognan – Grand Coin – Crêt Lognan – Col de Valbuche – Montaimont – Les Rieux – Col du Chaussy

Starting point: Col du Chaussy, 1533m, about 5km from Montaimont. Approach from the Maurienne A 43, Sortie 26 La Chambre, road up to the Col de la Madeleine, turn off right after about 5km. Or A 43 Pontamafrey exit, then the extremely winding D 77 via Montvernier and Montpascal.
Walking times: Col du Chaussy – Fontaine Bénite 1¾ hrs., Fontaine Bénite – Grand Coin 2¼ hrs., Grand Coin – Col de Valbuche ¾ hr., Col de Valbuche – Montaimont 2½ hrs., Montaimont – Les Rieux 1½ hrs., Les Rieux – Col du Chaussy 1 hr.; total time 9½ hrs.
Height difference: 1200m.
Grade: long ascent which demands a level of fitness. In the upper area there are a few tricky scree slopes to cross where sure-footedness and a lack of vertigo are essential, also on the steep descent. It's advisable to stay overnight in Montaimont. Leave your luggage in the hotel beforehand and then drive up in the car to the Col du Chaussy.
Food: in Montaimont.
Accommodation: Hotel Beauséjour, Montaimont (Chef-Lieu), ✆ 04 79 56 39 94, e-mail hotelbeausejour@voila.fr
Alternative: adventurous continuation of the ridge path: from the Col de Valbuche without paths ascend the steep grassy hillside to Pointe de Valbuche, 2629m; tracks again from here. Continue over Mollard des Boeufs, 2761m, to Bellachat, 2824m. There and back from the Col de Valbuche 4 hrs.
Map: IGN Top 25, sheet 3433 ET, St-Jean-de-Maurienne. St-Francois-Longchamp. Valmorel.
Tip: the Chemin des Hameaux offers a pleasant stroll and links the pretty hamlets of Montaimont. Info board, for example, at the church of Notre Dame de Beaurevers. If you like viewing the cultural heritage (patrimoine de Montaimont) like chapels, mills, local museums, find your way to Jean-Marc Pelissie who keeps the keys and can tell you many interesting things, ✆ 06 14 20 58 99.

Le Grand Coin – as the name already suggests, the large corner on the border ridge of the Tarentaise and the Maurienne, offers sensational views and an exciting ridge walk. From the summit you can see such famous peaks as Mont Blanc in the north, Grande Casse in the east, Pic de l'Etendard and the Aiguilles d'Arves in the south. The charming hamlets of Montaimont lie scattered at the foot of Grand Coin.
From the **Col du Chaussy**, 1533m, ascend the meadow path at the chapel, then go through a section of forest to the east to the meadows of Plan du Sapey. Traversing left you come to the **Fontaine Bénite** (walled spring). Continue southwards onto a mountain ridge, follow it for a short

way, then go to the right across the southern slope onto Crête de Coin Lognan. It's a tricky traverse just above to the right along hardly visible tracks across precipitous scree slopes, then ascending only gradually, go directly onto the ridge of Crêt Lognan which you follow to the right to **Grand Coin**, 2730m.

Return along the ridge to the cairn of the grassy summit of **Crêt Lognan**, 2696m. Continue without paths to the north down the ridge onto the **Col de Valbuche**, 2401m. Descend to the left down an unpleasantly steep and slippery scree path across the Grandes Combes, then more pleasantly across several streams and sloping meadows to the north, past the chalets of Closet, 1631m, to the road below Lac du Loup. Now either go along the road via Bonvillard back to the Col du Chaussy, which means a two hour walk along tarmac. Nicer, but longer – turn right into the little road which leads to the hamlet of **Le Loup**, 1481m, and along the Chemin des Hameaux via Taramur to **Montaimont**, 1102m, where you might stay overnight. Continue along the Chemin des Hameaux via **Les Rieux**, 1329m, and **Les Mottes**, 1392m, back to the starting point.

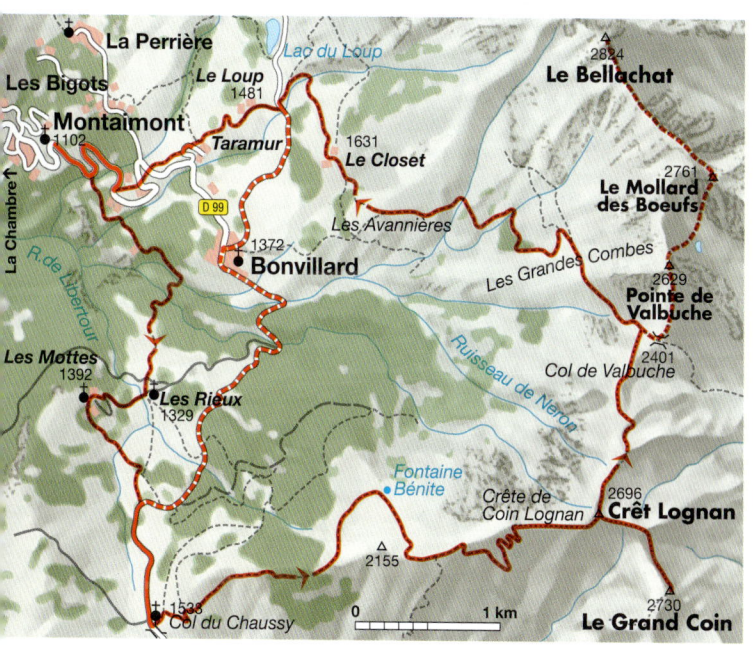

52 Rocher de Sarvatan, 2510m

Alpine walk through a strange 'sierra'

Longchamp – Col de Montjoie – Rocher de Sarvatan – Col de Sarvatan – Longchamp

Starting point: Télésiège de la Lauzière (ski lift), 1896m, above the ski station of Longchamp, 1650m, or on the first sharp left hand bend if you are coming from the Col de la Madeleine. Approach from La Chambre from the Maurienne or from Albertville along the N 90, exit 36, Feissons-sur-Isère.
Walking times: ski lift – Col de Montjoie 1½ hrs., Col de Montjoie – Col de Sarvatan 1½ hrs., to the summit of Rocher de Sarvatan and back ½ hr., Col de Sarvatan – ski lift 1 hr.; total time 4½ hrs.
Height difference: 750m.
Grade: easy climbing to the summit of Sarvatan (it's possible to go round, but then the grade is only 'red'). Short exposed section on the descent from the Col de Sarvatan. Usually patches of old snow at the start of June (walking poles are a good idea).
Food: none.
Map: IGN Top 25, sheet 3433 ET, St-Jean-de-Maurienne. St-Francois-Longchamp. Valmorel.

After you have just enjoyed the wonderful idyllic villages along the road coming down from the pass in the north and the view from the Col de la Madeleine of Mont Blanc which is truly amazing, your first impression of Longchamp, one of those ski stations excavated out of the earth, might be one of horror. Nevertheless, only a few hundred metres walk into the natural landscape and Longchamp is no longer of any significance. On this alpine walk you get impressions of the two different faces of the 30 kilometre long wall of the Lauzière mountain chain which is referred to geologically as a sierra. Its mountain sides in the east turn into lovely alpine pastures while, sometimes covered in dense woodland, they plummet dramatically over 2000m down into the Arc valley in the west. The Chartreuse and Bauges massifs can also be seen in the west beyond the Maurienne valley. In the south the Belledonne massif, Les Grandes Rousse with the Pic de l'Etendard, next to it on the left the three pinnacles of the Aiguilles d'Arves. In the east Cheval Noir, behind it the Vanoise glacier and Grande Casse. On the descent look back at the mountain ridge – La Louche Percée, the peak in the west, displays with its gaping rock window why it bears the amusing name of 'pierced soup spoon'.

On the Col de Montjoie.

From the car park go below the ski lift pylons of the **Télésiège de la Lauzière**, 1896m, and follow a clear, but unmarked path to the west uphill. A first signpost emerges in the boulder field of Grande Pierraille where you take the left hand fork towards the Col de Montjoie. From then on the path is waymarked in yellow.

You come to the small high plateau of La Platière, which is often confused with the actual pass. Continue westwards across the southern precipices of Roc Rouge, eventually up to the **Col de Montjoie**, 2253m.

A small mountain hut offers shelter. Do not follow the Chalet des Gardes signpost, go directly past the hut. After a short ascent, zigzag downhill, at times over the skillfully constructed walls of old avalanche barriers. At the first fork go right steeply up the bends of the western face of Rocher de Sarvatan until you reach the ridge, about 2420m, between La Grande Coutire and Sarvatan. If you do not feel confident about the easy climbing, cross directly over to the Col de Sarvatan, although this misses out on the best view. Otherwise go up the ridge over boulders to the summit of **Rocher de Sarvatan**, 2510m.

Return a few metres along the ridge and without paths down the scree of the steep northern hillside onto **Col de Sarvatan**, 2439m, to the hiking path. Steeply descend southeastwards through the cirque, then along the extensive boulder field of Grande Pieraille to the path that leads to the left back to the car park.

Index

A
Aiguille des Aimes 62
Aiguilles d'Arves 136
Albertville 28
Arènes, les 138
Aussois 112
Avérole 94

B
Basse du Gerbier 136
Bellecombe 102
Bessans 94, 96
Blockhaus des Têtes 28
Bonnenuit 134
Bonneval-sur-Arc 92
Bourg-St-Maurice 74
Bruyères, les 44

C
Camp des Rochilles 132
Cascade de la Reculaz 93
Celliers 38
Chal, la 148
Chalet de la Côte 68
Chalet de Rosoire 58
Chalet des Nants 54
Champagny-le-Haut 66
Champeney, le 30
Chapelle St-Barthélémy 120
Châtelard, le 76
Chenal 80
Cime de la Valette 138
Cirque de l'Arcelin 54
Cirque des Evettes 92
Cirque du Petit Marchet 54
Cirques de Pralognan 54
Coêtet, le 104
Col d'Aussois 114
Col de Chanrouge 46
Col de l'Iseran 90

Col de la Bauche de Mio 66
Col de la Croix de Fer 142
Col de la Croix des Frêtes 62
Col de la Galise 88
Col de la Grande Pierre 52
Col de la Grassaz 62
Col de la Louze 32
Col de la Madeleine 38
Col de la Masse 118
Col de la Rocheure 86
Col de la Valette 138
Col de la Vallée Etroite 44, 128
Col de la Vallette 54
Col de Lanserlia 102
Col de Montjoie 154
Col de Montséti 78
Col de Sarvatan 154
Col de Sollières 120
Col de Valbuche 152
Col des Aiguilles d'Arves 134
Col des Cerces 132
Col des Cyclotouristes 28
Col des Méandes 128
Col des Prés Nouveaux 138
Col des Rochilles 132
Col des Saulces 50
Col du Barbier 118
Col du Chaussy 152
Col du Coin 34
Col du Glandon 146
Col du Golet 52
Col du Gollet 40
Col du Grand Marchet 54
Col du Lac Noir 80
Col du Mône 50

Col du Palet 62
Col du Petit St-Bernard 74
Col du Plan Séry 62
Col du Rocher Blanc 80
Col du Sambuis 146
Col Nord des Lacs 142
Collet, le 100
Combe des Roches 50
Combe du Tépey 148
Crêt Lognan 152
Crête du Mont Charvet 52
Crève-Tête 40

D
Descente du Réposeu 148
Deux Ponts, les 138

E
Ecot, l' 92
Esseillon 108

F
Fontaine Bénite 152
Fort Charles-Albert 108
Fort Marie-Christine 108
Fort Victor-Emmanuel 108, 110
Forts de l'Esseillon 108
Frachettes, les 42

G
Glacier de la Savinaz 82
Glacier de Rochemelon 96
Glacier de St-Sorlin 142
Glacier des Fours 86
Gorge de la Reculaz 92
Gorges du Malpasset 88
Gorges St-Pierre 112
Grand Arc 30
Grand Coin 152
Grand Perron des Encombres 42

Grand Plan 38
Grand Prâlin 48, 50
Grande Maison, la 32
Gurraz, la 82

H

Haut du Pré 28
Hospice du Petit St-Bernard 74

L

Lac Blanc 58, 104
Lac Bramant 142
Lac d'Amour 34
Lac de l'Arpettaz 38
Lac de la Croix 146
Lac de la Plagne 70
Lac de la Sassière 84
Lac de Lou 44
Lac de Savine 122
Lac de Tuéda 46
Lac des Balmettes 150
Lac des Cerces 132
Lac du Branlay 38
Lac du Grand Ban 132
Lac du Mont Cenis 120
Lac du Mont Coua 46
Lac du Pêtre 48
Lac du Peyron 128
Lac du Retour 76
Lac du Sambuis 146
Lac Noir 78, 126
Lac Rond 132
Lac sans Fond 74
Lacs de la Tempête 32
Lacs de Pierre Blanche 44
Lacs des Lozières 104
Lacs Giaset 122
Lacs Merlet 48
Lacs Perrin 122
Laisonnay, le 62
Lancebranlette 74
Lanslebourg 100
Laval 34

Lavoir, le 128
Le Laital 138
Léchère, la 30
Longchamp 154

M

Manchet, le 86
Marret, le 30
Monal 80
Monolithe de Sardières 112
Mont Jovet 68
Mont Rond d'en bas 148
Mont Thabor 128
Mont, le 104
Montaimont 152

N

Notre-Dame du Pré 68

P

Parking de la Plate Form 68
Pas de la Coche 124
Passage du Retour 76
Perte du Ponturin 70
Petit Arc 30
Petit Col des Encombres 42
Petit Mont Blanc 50
Pic de Fremezan 150
Pierra Menta 34
Pierre aux Pieds 100
Plan d'Amont 114, 118
Plan d'Etache 126
Plan des Eaux 90, 124
Plan du Bouc 66
Plan du Lac 104
Plan Lachat 132
Plan, le 52
Planard de Combe Rousse 150
Planay, le 124
Planlebon 42
Plateau des Arponts 112
Pointe de l'Observatoire 114

Pointe de la Vélière 66
Pointe de Lanserlia 102
Pont de Chatelard 104
Pont de l'Oulietta 90
Pont de la Pêche 58
Pont du Diable 108
Pont St-Charles 88
Porte de Rosuel 70
Pralognan 52
Pré Bernard 138
Priots, les 42
Prioux, les 50, 54

R

Rateau d'Aussois 118
Refuge d'Ambin 124
Refuge d'Avérole 94
Refuge de Gittamelon 42
Refuge de l'Archeboc 78
Refuge de l'Arpont 104
Refuge de l'Etendard 142
Refuge de l'Orgère 118
Refuge de la Coire 34
Refuge de la Dent Parrachée 114
Refuge de la Glière 62
Refuge de la Martin 82
Refuge de Péclet Polset 58
Refuge de Pierre Larron 40
Refuge de Plaisance 62
Refuge de Prariond 88
Refuge de Presset 34
Refuge de Vallonbrun 100
Refuge des Aiguilles d'Arves 134
Refuge des Bachals 40
Refuge des Drayères 128
Refuge des Evettes 92
Refuge du Carro 90
Refuge du Cuchet 100
Refuge du Fond d'Aussois 114

Refuge du Fond des Fours 86
Refuge du Grand Plan 48
Refuge du Lac Blanc 104
Refuge du Mont Jovet 68
Refuge du Mont Thabor 128
Refuge du Petit Mont Cenis 122
Refuge du Plan du Lac 102, 104
Refuge du Ruitor 78
Refuge du Saut 46
Refuge Entre le Lac 70
Refuge la Fournache 114
Refuge le Logis des Fées 38
Rieux, les 152
Ritort 58

Roc de la Charbonnière 34
Roche Pourrie 28
Rochemelon 96
Rocher de Sarvatan 154
Rocher de Villeneuve 53

S
Saut, le 84
Savonne, la 78
Sentier Balcon de l'Arpont 104
Sentier des Bâtisseurs 108
Signal du Petit Mont Cenis 120
Sources de l'Arc 92
St-Colomban-des-Villards 150
Ste-Hélène-sur-Isère 30
St-Martin-de-Belleville 42

St-Sorlin d'Arves 136

T
Tête de Chat 135
Tougne, le 66
Tour de la Fourche 132
Trou de la Lune 112
Turra, la 112

V
Valfréjus 128
Vallée de Champagny 66
Vallée des Avals 48
Vallée des Encombres 42
Vallée du Morel 41
Vallée du Ribon 96
Vallon d'Ambin 124
Valmaure 148
Vaz, le 76
Via ferrata du Diable 110
Vincendières 94

GLOSSARY FOR MOUNTAIN WALKERS

l'abri	shelter	le lac	lake
l'aiguille	needle	la mairie	town hall
l'avalanche	avalanche	la marmotte	marmot
l'averses	precipitation	la montagne	mountain, mountain range
le barrage	dam	le mont	mountain
la barrière	barrier	la moraine	moraine
le belvédère	viewing point	la muraille	rock wall
le bois	forest, wood	le neige	snow
le bouquetin	ibex	le névé	snowfield, névé
la brèche	notch	l'orage	thunderstorm
le bussole	compass	le pas	mountain pass
le cairn	cairn	la passerelle	footbridge
la cascade	waterfall	le pic	peak
le chamois	chamois	le piolet	ice axe
le chemin	path	le pont	bridge
la chute de pierre	stonefall	le pré	meadow
la chute de serac	icefall	la randonnée	walk, hike
le cirque	cirque, valley basin	le refuge	refuge
le col	col, pass	la rivière	river
le collet	small pass	le rocher	rock
la combe	small high valley, hollow	le ruisseau	stream
la corde	rope	la rue	road, street
la crête	ridge, crest	la selle	col
la descente	descent	le sentier	path
l'eau potable	drinking water	le sommet	summit
l'étang	pool, lake	la source	source, spring
la falaise	steep rock face	le télésiege	chair lift
la fleur	flower	le télépherique	cable car
la fontaine	spring, well	la tête	summit
le glacier	glacier	le torrent	mountain stream
les gorges	gorge	la vallée	valley
le gouffre	ravine	le vallon	small valley, valley hollow
		VTT	mountain bike